BECOME YOUR BETTER SELF WITH POSITIVE DAILY AFFIRMATIONS

Boost Your Self-Esteem, Learn to Love Your Life and Make Everyday Special with Comforting and Motivational Daily Affirmations

TABLE OF CONTENT

INTRODUCTION 5

CHAPTER ONE DAILY POSITIVE AFFIRMATIONS TO START OFF YOUR DAY 7

CHAPTER TWO POSITIVE AFFIRMATIONS FOR LOVE . 17

CHAPTER THREE POSITIVE AFFIRMATIONS FOR HEALTH 26

CHAPTER FOUR POSITIVE AFFIRMATIONS FOR FINANCES 35

CHAPTER FIVE POSITIVE AFFIRMATIONS FOR BUSINESS 43

CHAPTER SIX POSITIVE AFFIRMATIONS FOR CONFIDENCE 52

CHAPTER SEVEN POSITIVE AFFIRMATIONS FOR PEACE OF MIND 60

CHAPTER EIGHT POSITIVE AFFIRMATIONS FOR SPIRITUALITY 69

CHAPTER NINE POSITIVE AFFIRMATIONS FOR THE CAREER MINDED 79

CHAPTER TEN POSITIVE AFFIRMATIONS FOR CREATIVITY 90

CHAPTER ELEVEN POSITIVE AFFIRMATIONS FOR WOMEN 97

CHAPTER TWELVE POSITIVE AFFIRMATIONS FOR MEN 107

CHAPTER THIRTEEN POSITIVE AFFIRMATIONS FOR TEENAGERS 116

CHAPTER FOURTEEN POSITIVE AFFIRMATIONS FOR PREGNANCY 124

CHAPTER FIFTEEN POSITIVE AFFIRMATIONS FOR TOUGH TIMES 134

CHAPTER SIXTEEN POSITIVE AFFIRMATIONS FOR WEIGHT LOSS 143

CHAPTER SEVENTEEN POSITIVE AFFIRMATIONS FOR MANIFESTING DESIRES 153

CHAPTER EIGHTEEN POSITIVE AFFIRMATIONS FOR MEDITATIONS 162

CHAPTER NINETEEN POSITIVE AFFIRMATIONS FOR BIRTHDAYS 171

CHAPTER TWENTY POSITIVE AFFIRMATIONS FOR THE TRAVELLER 180

CHAPTER TWENTY-ONE POSITIVE AFFIRMATIONS ABOUT EMOTIONS 186

INTRODUCTION

There is a general saying in life; that you are what you eat. If life has taught me anything, it is the humble knowledge that we are a sum total of our experiences and our experiences are dictated by the words that we speak. Many people would find it difficult to accept this simple truth and this is because most people fall into two spectrums. Those who have resigned themselves to the dictates of fate and those who struggle daily to control their fate.

The first set of people believe that the Universe is solely responsible for whatever we go through in life. And if you question their logic, they have this belief that the Universe is a being of immerse power and strength with little to no care for mankind. This being just does what he or she pleases and acts impulsively to satisfy their whim. Which is why a person would be born into a life of hardship, toil their way to the top and just at the point when they are about to reap the rewards of their labor, the person's life is cut short by a totally random event like a rock falling out of the sky or a quick ailment. In the same way, you have a person born into a completely lavish lifestyle and for the rest of their life, they do not have to toil a single day. The contrasts between these two personalities and the unfairness of it all is what the first group of people use to allude to a supernatural being that is sometimes called the Universe.

The second group of people have a firm grip on their destiny and they refuse to relinquish control to anyone or anything…human or supernatural. Their lives are sequential order of events managed to the point of obsession by time. For them, life happens but they are going to do everything in their power to ensure that life happens the way that they want it. Sometimes, things do not go exactly according to their plan. This can be extremely frustrating for them and if care is not taking, it can cause a deep psychological break down. When that doesn't happen, they piece themselves pack together and attack life with the same tenacious vigor that characterizes everything that they do. The problem with them is that anything that doesn't fit into their plan is quickly brushed aside or thrown under the bus. Their experiences are limited to their plans.

Life is meant to be lived with limitless possibilities. You can't control what happens to you but you can control how you perceive the experiences you have had. In fact, you can go a step further to redefine how your life is shaped by those experiences. The best part of this is that you don't have to appeal to any supreme being or take permission from anyone to live your life to the fullest. By speaking positive words, you attract positive experiences into your life and even when tragedy occurs (because this is life), your words can shape exactly how that tragedy can affect you. It would either shape you or break you. This is a subconscious choice that you must make everyday and without realizing this, we make this choice with the words that we speak. In this book, you would find positive words of affirmations that can be adapted to suit every situation. From sunrise to sunset, through every season in your life, fill your mouth with words that elevate you and deliver to you, experiences that make life worth living.

Be inspired to live better every day!

CHAPTER ONE

DAILY POSITIVE AFFIRMATIONS TO START OFF YOUR DAY

1. Today is going to be a wonderful day
2. I open my heart, my mind and my body to amazing experiences
3. My today is better than my yesterday
4. Every day and in every way, I am getting better and better
5. Today, I am abundantly joyful and happy
6. I am full of gratitude for my life this morning
7. I find beauty and joy in all the things I do today
8. I am clear, untouched, and unharmed by all the negative experiences of yesterday.
9. My life today is a joy. I relax easily and open myself up to delightful surprises
10. I permit myself to live a life that is joyful and filled with love, fun and friendship
11. Right now, I choose love, joy and freedom
12. I open my heart and allow wonderful gifts of life to flow into me
13. Everything in my life is exactly as it should be
14. As the morning glory blossoms in the morning, my life is blossoming in perfection
15. Today, I am radiating with loving kindness and life mirrors this back to me
16. Like the morning sun, I am full of positive life-giving energy.
17. I experience total freedom from the burdens of my past.
18. I refuse to live like a victim this beautiful day
19. Yesterdays experiences has lost its hold on me

20. Today, I live in the consciousness of who I am in this present moment
21. I forgive myself for the mistakes of yesterday and set myself free from guilt.
22. I am abundantly blessed with treasures and gifts that warm my heart
23. I use my gifts and blessings lovingly when I have influence over others
24. I fill my heart positive musings that amplify my zest for life
25. I embrace wisdom, knowledge and understanding today
26. I am a powerful being and I bask in the knowledge of who I am
27. I resist and shut out any negative force that seeks to diminish my light
28. As the world awakens to the brightness of the sun, so do people come to my rising
29. The relationships that I need to thrive are locating me today
30. I welcome love and romance into my life.
31. I feel my center with light and love
32. My life is open to people who reflect the same degree of light and love
33. I am surrounded by loving and supportive relationships
34. I deserve love and I get it in abundance.
35. I am loved, loving and lovable.
36. I am building and nurturing healthy relationships with my family and friends
37. I am blessed with an incredible family and wonderful friends.
38. I give out love and it is returned to me multiplied many folds.
39. Good things are happening throughout today.
40. No matter what happens today, then end result would be joy
41. I am filled with love, hope and confidence about my future
42. I greet each second of today with enthusiasm and hope.
43. I am awake to the opportunities that are present in this day.

44. If I falter, I get positive reminders that my life is filled with joy and love.
45. I do not live in the fear of making mistakes
46. There is a magical element to me, and my life is full of serendipity
47. My thoughts and feelings are positively nourishing.
48. I am present and conscious of every beautiful moment.
49. I see beauty in every person I meet.
50. People treat me with kindness and respect, and I treat them the same.
51. I am surrounded by peaceful people.
52. I bring peace to the people who encounter me today
53. My environment is calm and supportive.
54. I am the architect of my life. I am the creator of my reality.
55. I envelop myself in self-acceptance today
56. I choose to believe that I am supported and loved by the Universe
57. I am surrounded by abundance.
58. I am healthy, energetic and optimistic.
59. I am overflowing with happiness, joy and satisfaction
60. I transcend every form of negativity.
61. I proclaim that I can, and I will achieve greatness today
62. I know that everything happens for a reason; everything leads to something positive.
63. I let go of any grudges I am holding against myself or another person.
64. I am forgiving. My compassion replaces anger with love
65. I am at peace with my past.
66. I make the choice to reflect love, happiness, grace and positivity
67. I am patient, diplomatic and tolerant.
68. I am grateful for the miracles in my life.
69. No matter what, the universe supports me in every possible way.

70. The experiences in my life today helps me to grow.
71. Today I lay the foundation for a wonderful future.
72. I am sowing seeds with fruitful dividends
73. I am safe and protected by divinity in all my goings and comings
74. Danger and harm are not featured in my day
75. All the resources I need to thrive are made available to me
76. Everything I seek can be found within.
77. I set myself free from and anxiety and fears about the future
78. I am significant. I contribute to the advancement of humankind.
79. Today, my footprints in the sands of time are etched deeper.
80. This day will bring me nothing absolute joy, fulfillment and happiness.
81. I have all it takes to make this day relevant and memorable
82. I face any difficulties in this day with courage and endurance.
83. I am excited to witness the making of the best years of my life.
84. I am excited about the amazing journeys I am going to take today.
85. I am mentally and emotionally prepared for the challenges of the day.
86. Today I fill myself with positive energy.
87. I am calm and patient in the face of any crisis today
88. I am filled with confidence and positivity at the thought of facing today
89. The blessings of this new day energize me.
90. This morning, I make the conscious choice to be happy
91. The potential in my day is not lost to me
92. Today is a blessing and a gift that I will not waste.
93. I trust my inner wisdom to guide me throughout my day.
94. I avoid self-doubt today by not comparing myself to others.
95. I am full of potential and today, I recognize it

96. I receive the people I meet today with an open heart and an open mind.
97. I will not compare myself to others.
98. Today I feel healthy and strong, physically, emotionally, and mentally.
99. Today I will accomplish greater things than I did yesterday
100. Today, I am triumphant in my dealings

ACTIONABLE AFFIRMATIONS FOR YOUR DAY

1. Happiness is my birthright. This morning, I am using happiness as my default setting.
2. I free myself from greed and choose instead to feel joy and contentment at this moment right now.
3. I am not sad or depressed, instead, I am feeling happy and enthusiastic about life.
4. I can tap into a wellspring of inner happiness today I wish therefore I am optimistic.
5. I inspire others to be happy as well by allowing myself to be happy
6. I have fun with all my endeavors, even the most mundane activity brings me joy.
7. I look at the world around me and can't help but smile and feel joy.
8. I find joy and pleasure in the simplest things in life.
9. My sense of humor is active, and I love to share this to bring laughter to others.
10. My heart is overflowing with joy, nothing threatens my joy today/
11. Life is happening in this moment and I choose to live in the consciousness of this
12. I will not falter today because trust myself and know my inner wisdom is my best guide.

13. My name has value because I have integrity. I am totally reliable. I do what I say.
14. Today, I put aside all irrational thoughts. I act from a place of personal security.
15. Today I will not settle for less because I fully accept myself and know that I am worthy of great things in life.
16. I will not wallow in poor opinion of myself. I boldly choose to be proud of myself.
17. I am not afraid of what today holds as I am willing to accept and embrace all experiences, even unpleasant ones.
18. I remove any dark clouds hanging over me and fill my mind with positive and nourishing thoughts.
19. At the end of today, I will I rest in happiness when I go to sleep, knowing with my entire being that all is well in my world.
20. I choose to use my time better by assessing/ myself and my actions rather than judging the deeds or misdeeds or other people in my life
21. I am making bold choices without fear today. Choices that reflect the beauty and light that resides within me.
22. This morning, I embrace the chance to be better than I was yesterday. I am making only the best decisions for my life today.
23. I am choosing to maintain a positive attitude today despite any hurdles that come my way because I know that I have what it takes to succeed.
24. In this moment, I am exactly where I need to be in life. I welcome the challenges and opportunities that I am facing today, and I choose to learn and grow.
25. To harvest a better tomorrow, I only plant positive seeds in the world today. I do not waste one precious moment in anger, hatred, or envy.

26. I am not living my life passively with no purpose. I am on earth for a reason, and I am committed to living a positive life and being a positive influence on others.
27. I choose to take responsibility for my own happiness today. I do not allow anyone else to have the power over how I feel because I am in control.
28. I see my true nature. I am beautiful and I look and feel radiant both inside and outside.
29. I recognize the talent that I have and knowing I have so much to offer the world, I refuse to be mediocre.
30. I refuse to waste my talent today. I am a person of excellence therefore, I am putting my 100% in all I do
31. I keep the energy revitalizing today therefore I will not be engaging in activities like that drain me emotionally like gossiping, bullying and so on.
32. I have a winning mentality so even if I fail at something today, I choose not to be defined by it
33. My path to the life that I hope for is revealed to me and I do not have to hurt or harm anyone to get to my destination
34. My vision for my life today is as clear as the sun, I am not stumbling around in the dark to achieve my goals today
35. I trust in the provisions made available by the universe therefore I do not live in fear for the security of my life, my family and my properties.
36. Today, I make enlightened decisions about my life and I no longer fear for the consequences of my actions because I am sowing the right seeds
37. The words that I speak today are graceful and pleasing to the ear so that even in anger, my words remain pleasant and nurturing
38. As clear as clouds are on a sunny day, so are my thoughts. I am not confused or double minded about the choices I make

39. This light that burns brightly on the inside of me will not be hidden from the world. I choose to shine brightly for the world to see
40. I love myself and like myself. I choose to focus on my positive qualities and how I can use them to improve myself and the world.
41. I am living my own version of happiness today. My joy is sourced from within and has nothing to do with anyone else. I am happy for anyone else who is happy and other people are happy for me.
42. I accept that I am not perfect. And if I do something wrong, I will go back and find another way. I create a new course of action. I do not stop.
43. Today, I am ready to commit to the life that I dream of, and the world works along with me to help attain my vision.
44. Today, I take the first of many steps towards attaining my goals and the rest comes naturally.
45. Today, I choose to use the time I have in a way that is in line with my values and goals. Rather than complaining about not having enough time today
46. I refuse to be idle this wonderful day. I am making a conscious effort to make the best of every moment I am given today.
47. I trust my own wisdom and intuition to guide me in my productive endeavors. I know what is best for me and I surround myself with people who want the best for me.
48. On this day of blessings and abundance, I refuse to believe that my options are limited. The opportunities coming my way are limitless.
49. Today, I am ready to create more success in my life and I refuse to entertain any excuses that will slow me down. I am productive and focused on attaining results.
50. Today I am elevated to greater heights

AFFIRMATIONS FOR THE SUCCESS OF THE DAY

51. I am setting up my mind for greatness today
52. The light of the sun touches every area of my life that has been experiencing darkness
53. I feel the pulse of the universe as I set out today
54. I am pulsating with positive energy for greatness
55. I do not have a mentality of failure today. I have blessings and lessons
56. The winds and the atmosphere are favorable for me today
57. I am alive to the goodness of this day
58. I tap into the source of happiness to get me through this day
59. I will not be hindered by the failures of others
60. I welcome blessings in unexpected places
61. I am revitalized from the inside out for the day ahead
62. My way has been made straight for me, so I sail through the day effortlessly
63. I am resourceful
64. I am determined
65. I am succeeding without any restrictions
66. I am breaking glass ceilings without fear or hesitation
67. I am accomplishing something great today
68. I have ordained this morning as the birthing point of my glory
69. Life is so much easier for me today
70. Today, I refuse to be invisible. My feelings and efforts are recognized
71. Today is the day that I will be celebrated by my peers
72. There is a restoration of broken relationships today
73. I know the right thing to say and do at any point in time
74. Today, I am delivered into a joyful experience that uplifts me

75. The seeds that bring about the permanence of happiness in my life are planted today
76. Just as the night transforms to daytime, I am radically transformed into greatness
77. I refuse to ponder on the things that I lack or do not have
78. Today, my joy knows no bounds
79. As I speak these words of affirmation, I feel the light radiating throughout my entire being
80. I am truly delighted about the changes that are coming today
81. I speak order and organization into this day
82. There will be no chaos in this day and even when chaos presents itself, I will make order out of it
83. I am accomplishing great feats today
84. I do not have the words to describe how amazing the gift of today is to me
85. The environment that I live and conduct all of my affairs is conducive enough for me to thrive
86. Today, I rise out of the ashes of the past
87. I am taking on my day from a place of comfort and wisdom
88. I am capable of handling everything that comes my way today
89. I do not falter under the weight of the events of today
90. I am constantly reminded of the greatness within at different points throughout today
91. Today, I experience the freedom to create my ideal reality for the future I desire. I have a choice in every situation that I face. There is nothing that can get between me and my best self.

CHAPTER TWO

POSITIVE AFFIRMATIONS FOR LOVE

1. I feel pure love within me - and all around me
2. I embrace the blessings of love and romance into my life.
3. The relationship that I am in is loving and supportive
4. I am made for love and I get it in abundance.
5. I am truly loved, very loving and 100% lovable.
6. I have been blessed with an incredible family and wonderful friends.
7. I give out genuine love and the universe returns this to me multiplied many folds.
8. I am constantly radiating love and other person reflects love back to me.
9. I love myself enough to recognize healthy love when I receive it
10. My romantic relationship is healthy, long-lasting and full of love.
11. My partner is kind, compassionate and understanding in our relationship
12. My partner is very physically, emotionally, sexually and spiritually attracted to me.
13. I am with my ideal partner and we share a life full of love.
14. My life is full of love and I find it everywhere I go.
15. My relationship is rooted in love, and my partner and I are perfectly matched.
16. There is a deep understanding between my partner and me.
17. Forgiveness and compassion are the foundation of my romantic relationship.

18. My words towards others are always kind and loving, and in return, I hear kindness and love from others.
19. Every day of my life is filled with genuine love.
20. All forms of communication between my partner and I are established in love.
21. I know I am amazing, and I am worthy of true love.
22. My personality attracts the right kind of person for me
23. I know that I face each day with the support and love of my partner and the people who love me
24. All my relationships are nurturing and healthy because they are based in love and compassion.
25. I attract love and light into my life because I am a beacon of love and compassion.
26. I have a vibrant personality, and everyone sees how much joy and love I have for life.
27. I experience positivity in all my relationships as they are filled with love and compassion.
28. I see the good in other people and I acknowledge their efforts to be their best.
29. I always find opportunities to be kind and caring at every turn.
30. I am genuinely in love with myself and feel great about myself.
31. I accept myself and the love I have for myself is unconditional.
32. My heart is always open to forging new relationships. I am kind to every person I meet.
33. I surround myself with love, so I attract kind people.
34. I love people unconditionally and I do so without hesitation.
35. I dwell in love. I do good deeds and my efforts are appreciated by those around me.
36. I am accompanied by love everywhere I go.
37. Love, forgiveness and understanding is the very foundation of my relationships.

38. I have the capacity to give and receive love equally.
39. I accept my partner wholesomely and unconditionally.
40. I am treasured for who I really am in my relationships
41. My marriage/relationship is waxes stronger, deeper and more loving with every single day.
42. My friendships are meaningful, supportive and rewarding to me and the people involved
43. My friends know and love me for who I am.
44. I am accepting of others and it helps me to establish long-lasting friendships.
45. I attract positive people into with whom I quickly forge lifetime bonds.
46. I surround myself with friends who genuinely care about my wellbeing and treat me well
47. My partner and I share a deep and powerful love for each other that keeps us connected.
48. I wholly trust, respect and admire my partner and I see the best in him/her.
49. I love my partner exactly how he/she is and enjoy his/her unique qualities without conditions.
50. My partner and I share emotional intimacy daily through activities we both enjoy.
51. I have healthy boundaries with my partner, and they respect it.
52. My partner and I have fun together and find new ways to enjoy our time together.
53. My partner and I communicate openly and resolve conflict peacefully and respectfully.
54. I am the most authentic version of myself in my love relationship.
55. I am able to communicate my desires and needs clearly and share with my partner.
56. I want the best for my partner and my actions reflect my desire for my partner

57. I easily go out of my way to support my partner to achieve their goals
58. I am grounded in love and empathy
59. I am worthy of love and trust in my relationships and friendships.
60. I actively nurture healthy relationships with the people I love.
61. I bring joy to those around me.
62. I am grateful for all who love and care for me.
63. My friendships are important to me.
64. My love and loyalty are not called to question at any point
65. I know how important it is to just listen to others.
66. My friends love and respect me.
67. My relationships bring me joy.
68. I have an inner fountain of love that I continuously draw from
69. My love tank is consistently replenished
70. Love is not a foreign concept to me
71. I have learned how to speak the love language of my partner fluently
72. I am not confounded by the actions or inactions of others in my relationship
73. The love that I give is not dependent on any external source
74. I have the ability to recognize genuine love
75. I do not love people to the point of obsession
76. My partner does not feel caged by the love that I show them
77. The love that I give is strong and healthy
78. I am capable of loving people past their flaws and errors
79. The negative love experiences of my past do not define my present relationships
80. My heart is big enough to embrace the people in my circle and beyond
81. I am compassionate and giving in the way that I love
82. I recognize the worth of the people in my love
83. I open up myself to communicate effective in my relationships

84. I do not shut out my partner or the people that genuinely care about me
85. I appreciate the love that I receive, and I show my appreciation appropriately
86. The love that I have is not a bargaining chip in any of my relationships
87. I have a unique insight into the needs of my partner
88. I do not betray my partner at any point in our relationship
89. I do not expect perfection from my partner, but I love him/her perfectly
90. The love that I give is rooted in the right things
91. I am secure in the love of my partner and vice versa
92. I fall in love with myself each passing day
93. My expression of love is not limited by my experiences
94. I have no desire to validate the love I feel to anyone but me
95. I love myself enough to leave toxic relationships
96. I embrace the differences between myself and my partner
97. My love for my partner is consistently renewed in committed relationships
98. I am ready to put in the work that it takes to keep my relationships alive
99. I do not speak words that destroy people
100. I am a nurturer and my love cause people to blossom
101. I am patient, kind and understanding
102. I do not make assertions people without verifying the authenticity of that statement
103. I give of myself freely without conditions or expectations
104. My love is not dependent on the circumstances surrounding me
105. I am capable of loving the people in my life through good and bad times
106. My relationship is built on shared principles that provide a solid foundation
107. I have a shared intimacy with my partner that is deep

108. I do not hold grudges or hold past sins against my partner
109. My expectation of love is rooted in tangible principles
110. I value loyalty and therefore, I am a loyal friend
111. I have the courage to apologize when I have wronged the people, I care about
112. I completely forgive people who have wronged me in turn
113. I am discreet about the personal details that people confide in me
114. I do not betray the trust of my friend, partner or family
115. With each passing day, I am presented with an opportunity to grow in my relationship
116. The love that I share with my partner in marriage is divine
117. I am not a loner, I have the ability to make good friends
118. I am an appreciative person
119. There is enough room in my heart for love
120. I am selfless but that does not mean that I love myself less
121. I hold myself accountable for the relationships that I have
122. In times of disagreement, I communicate without humiliating
123. My partner and I grow together. We do not grow apart
124. There is room for positive growth in all my relationships
125. In my marriage, my partner and I aspire for attainable things
126. I am very content in this relationship
127. My relationships are characterized by love, happiness and genuine affection
128. I am moved by the pains of my partner and I actively try to stop the hurt
129. I am not vindictive in any of my relationships
130. There are no dangerous secrets between me and my partner
131. The environment in my marriage makes it easy to talk about everything
132. My partner's happiness is independent of me and vice versa

133. My marriage is set up for the long haul
134. My relationship is a haven for me, and I find peace in it
135. I am mentally and emotionally strong to weather the tides and seasons of my marriage
136. My partner is mentally and emotionally strong to weather the times and seasons of this marriage
137. I distance myself from toxic people and toxic relationships
138. I am supportive and progressive in all of my relationships
139. My love is not restricted to a few but welcoming to all
140. My partner and I age gracefully but our love remains new
141. My marriage is everything my partner and I envisioned for ourselves
142. I am articulate without being hurtful in my communication with my partner
143. My partner and I are on the same page emotionally, financially and spiritually
144. My home is a harbor from the outside world that is full of peace, love and harmony
145. I am comfortable in my relationship
146. I am deeply connected to my partner in the ways that matter
147. Love is not an elusive concept for me
148. I am unwavering in the trust I have for my partner
149. My partner gives me no reason to question the trust I have for them
150. I am completely open to my partner. I do not hide parts of myself from them
151. There is order in my relationship
152. Regret is a foreign concept in all my relationships
153. I deal with loss in a healthy manner
154. If I experience loss, I do not hide from the grief but I am not overwhelmed by it
155. This union is a successful and progressive union
156. I fall in love with my partner every single day

157. I am fervent and consistent in my affirmations of love
158. I never miss the chance to tell my partner how much I love them
159. I never miss the chance to declare my affections for the people I love
160. I belong wholly to my beloved as my beloved is mine
161. I prioritize the relationships that I have
162. I do not take the people that I care about for granted
163. I do not sit by and watch another human suffer
164. I show empathy and compassion when they are needed
165. I am reliable and dependable in relationships
166. I am moved to show acts of kindness on a daily basis
167. I am not discriminatory in my relationships
168. My friends find it very easy to confide in me because they know that I am discreet
169. I have genuine respect and love for the people in my life
170. I do not feel bitter or jealous about the successes of my friends
171. I am letting go of bad habits that influence my love negatively
172. I am embracing good habits that nurture and grow my love
173. I am a blessing to the people in my world
174. I don't try to impress people with my love. I simply express it
175. I work in the consciousness of the divine love that I have within
176. I instinctively know how to love the people I come in contact with
177. The in my heart for my partner is not something I have to labor painfully for
178. Love comes into my life effortlessly
179. My love is like the stars at night. Even in the darkness of life it shines through

180. I am not unreasonable in love. My head and heart are involved
181. My love does not discriminate but it is not blind either
182. Every good thing that has been said about love is a daily experience for me
183. I conquer every negative stereotype about love and transcend any unhealthy expectation concerning love
184. My self-love game is top notch. I love myself in the most beautiful ways
185. I surround myself with the good kind of love, but I can always look inward and find the love I need
186. The size of my wallet does not determine the degree of my love
187. I always find creative and positive ways to express my love
188. I will always feel loved no matter what
189. I do my part in making the world a more loving and forgiving place
190. The love I have for humans is extended to the world as a whole
191. I care for and love the plants and animals that I have been blessed to know and nurture
192. I am not unkind to people regardless of station or status
193. I surround myself with people I love, and care about, but also take time to nurture my relationship with myself.

CHAPTER THREE

POSITIVE AFFIRMATIONS FOR HEALTH

1. I deserve to be healthy and feel good about myself
2. I am full of energy and vitality and my mind is calm and peaceful.
3. Every day, I am getting healthier and stronger.
4. I honor my body by treating myself to healthy meals
5. I attend to the needs of my body; trusting the signals that it sends me.
6. I manifest perfect health by consciously making smart choices.
7. I engage in healthy stimulation throughout my day.
8. I eat healthy, nutritious food during my lunch break and my body is grateful, granting me energy and good health in return.
9. I radiate success and health.
10. I develop healthy habits that support my health journey
11. I wake up in good health daily
12. I am grateful for how effectively and efficiently my body works.
13. I embrace the shape of my body and I find it beautiful and appealing.
14. I only make healthy and nourishing eating choices.
15. I take care of my body and exercise every day.
16. My body is healthy and full of energy.
17. My body is a constant marvel to me
18. My body is filled with healing energy every time I inhale.
19. I amazed by the things I can accomplish with my body

20. I am very grateful and happy that I weigh ___ (fill in with desired weight).
21. I crave healthy, nutritious foods.
22. I am surrounded by people who positively motivate my health choices
23. I love the taste of fruits and vegetables.
24. I am in love with every curve in my body.
25. Every organ in my body is working the way it was designed to work
26. I am grateful for the life force and energy that runs through my body.
27. Everything I think, say and do makes me healthier.
28. I feel safe and comfortable in my body.
29. No food is off limits to me. However, I eat in moderation
30. Everything I do is fun, healthy and exciting.
31. I crave new but healthy experiences.
32. I eat the foods that I desire but I practice portion control
33. Every day I'm getting healthier.
34. I am full of vitality.
35. Every meal that I take is consciously prepared with the needs of my body in mind
36. I take good care of my body and eat a healthy, well-balanced diet.
37. My body is a holy temple. I keep it clean and maintain its functionality.
38. I exercise regularly and strengthen my body.
39. Every cell in my body vibrates with energy and health.
40. I observe my emotions without getting physically affected by them
41. I nourish my body with healthy food.
42. All of my body systems are functioning perfectly.
43. Every single cell in my body is working as it was designed to
44. My body is healing, and I feel better and better every day.
45. I enjoy exercising my body and strengthening my muscles.

46. With every breath out, I release stress out of my body.
47. I indulge in practices that promote healing
48. I send love and healing to every organ of my body.
49. I breathe deeply, exercise regularly and feed only good nutritious food to my body.
50. I pay attention and listen to what my body needs for health and vitality.
51. I sleep soundly and peacefully and awaken feeling rested and energetic.
52. I am surrounded by people who encourage and support healthy choices.
53. I approve of myself and love myself deeply and completely.
54. My confidence, self-esteem and inner wisdom are increasing with each day.
55. I have sound health teachers all around me
56. I have peace of mind concerning my health
57. My body may not meet the worldly standard for beauty, but I am beautiful
58. I don't engage in exercises or activities that jeopardize my health
59. My body is a constantly enjoying daily health benefits
60. I have the resources needed to stay healthy and in good shape
61. I have the right kind of health information to stay in peak performance
62. The aging of my body occurs slowly so that I look younger than my actual age
63. Despite my genetic history, I am a picture of perfect health
64. I am not plagued by the medical history of those who came before me
65. I will not be shamed into making choices that do not reflect my health decisions
66. I am constantly alert to my body and I listen to its needs
67. I do not take short cuts to attaining the healthy lifestyle that I desire

68. I am a vision of health in motion
69. I am confident that I am always in a state of good health
70. I enjoy the daily benefits of being healthy
71. I am not worried about my health as the universe works to ensure that I am fine
72. I take delight in health focused activities
73. There is no lack of vital health information to me
74. I intuitively know the things that are good for my body and I take the steps to follow through on those things
75. My eyes are open to the daily benefits that surround me
76. I am grateful and appreciative of the good health that I have
77. I am programmed to engage in activities that are beneficial to my health
78. I do not fall for the gimmicks of fake health experts
79. I successfully stay on track with all my health goals
80. My vibrancy is not diminished by the day
81. My heart is strong enough to support the needs of my body
82. My lungs take in the right amount of air needed to replenish my body
83. I am revitalized from the inside out
84. When it comes to my health I don't just live, I thrive
85. My health is getting better and better
86. My family would not receive any negative news concerning my health
87. I am an example of picture-perfect health
88. My bones are strong enough to support the weight of my body
89. I refuse to procrastinate about the healthy needs of my body
90. I avoid people or situations that compromise my overall health
91. The state of my health transcends the physical
92. I am emotionally and mentally healthy too
93. I have healthier ways to cope with stress

94. I do not eat my feelings, instead, I discover healthier outlets for them
95. I know my health triggers and I take conscious steps to avoid them
96. I do not live in the shadow of whatever medical condition ails me
97. I am proactive about the choices that I make
98. I make health goals that are critical but attainable
99. I have the right kind of support needed to keep me on track with my health goals
100. I am not fazed by the prospects of tomorrow. Things are good
101. All the organs and systems in my body are working in unison for the betterment of my body
102. There is no shortage of ideas on how to keep me healthy
103. I take my health and its care seriously
104. My health providers are heaven sent and they go above and beyond duty to keep me in good shape
105. The science needed to keep me healthy has been invented
106. In the event of frailty, my body's healing process is fast tracked
107. There are no limitations to what I can achieve with my body
108. What was meant to be a disability for me is channeled into laying the foundation for my strength
109. I am a multi-purpose being. All my senses are engaged therefore, the shutting down of one part does not mean I lose that function completely
110. Accidents happen, but I am in complete control of what happens afterwards
111. I expect good news concerning my health today
112. Any cell growth that is contrary to the norm and has the potential to compromise my health, I stop it right now
113. Everything in my body is as it should be

114. My paths will never cross with that of anyone who seeks to profit off my health needs at my expense without proffering real solutions
115. I am mentally competent to make decisions regarding my health
116. I am physically fit and mentally strong
117. I am proactive in anything that has to do with my health
118. My health is stable
119. I find fun and innovative ways to include a balanced diet and exercise into my daily routine
120. I am mastering the art of living healthy daily
121. My kitchen and fridge are a reflection of the healthy choices I have decided to make
122. My body is weaned off those harmful things that I crave
123. The state of my health is not defined by my age
124. I am constantly doing the best to stay in shape, and I do this effortlessly
125. Any addiction I have that compromises my health is stopped today
126. I am better today than I was yesterday
127. My commitment to staying in good health is displayed in my actions
128. I hold myself accountable for my health and I do not wait on other people to attain my health goals
129. I deliberately surround myself with people who share the same goals with me
130. There is no shortage of new and exciting ways to remain in good health
131. I am willing to invest in my health
132. The laws of the land and the laws of the universe are aligning together to work in favor of my wellbeing
133. The health policies that are being formulated are in my favor
134. I get the help that I need exactly when I need it

135. I am daily inspired and motivated to be healthy
136. My thoughts are centered on healthy
137. I am thinking of vitality in my waking moments
138. I do not accept any condition that does not reflect good health
139. The divine plan is for me to be in good health and I align my thoughts with this
140. My words, my thoughts and actions are a reflect of the perfect state of my health
141. I possess and claim the healing power that my body needs to thrive
142. My body is conditioned to be in good health
143. I am conscious of the vitality of my body
144. Good health is my birthright and I claim it
145. There is no limit to the abundant healing power that is flowing in my body
146. I do not accept any diagnosis of "incurable" disease
147. There is a solution for whatever my body is going through
148. I am perfectly whole and healthy
149. My physical stamina today is getting stronger
150. In areas where my body is ailing, I speak healing to those parts
151. Divine healing finds expression in my body
152. I am not held captive or hostage by any ailment
153. My body conforms to the words that I speak over it
154. I always speak positively concerning my health
155. I am completely healthy in body, mind and spirit
156. Wherever there is a disconnection or malfunction of an organ, cell or system in my body, I speak restoration over it
157. My body is strong. My body is agile. My body is a power house
158. I constantly defy medical expectations in a good way
159. I enjoy the pleasures of good food and food has always been good to my body

160. I have a positive attitude towards my body
161. My body is positively exceptional
162. I don't push my body beyond its limits
163. I eat and enjoy all types of food
164. Every exchange of breath restores vitality to my body
165. The cells in my body intelligently work together to revitalize my body
166. I develop the right partnerships that help promote my health
167. Anything that will compromise my health is positioned far away from me
168. Everything is working together for my wellbeing
169. Healing is my daily portion in life
170. Good health is a constant presence in my life
171. I am not moved by the diagnosis of doctors and physicians, I know that I am healthy
172. I am a manifestation of the divine healing power within
173. My intuition guides me on the right choice to make pertaining to my health
174. My home is a hub of vitality and goodness
175. When I close my eyes to sleep, my body's self-healing system is reactivated
176. I wake up refreshed, revitalized and fully restored
177. The words that I speak over my body are filled with life
178. Pain and disease are a rarity for me
179. I always have good news about my health
180. I am immune to any air, water or food borne virus that compromises my health
181. My immune system is in excellent condition
182. I do not fall victim to any plague or virus
183. My health is divine, and it is not conditioned by what is going on around me
184. I have peace of mind regarding my health

185. I am undoing any harm brought on my body by years of bad habits
186. I receive positive feedback for the efforts I put into staying healthy
187. My immune system is very strong and can deal with any kind of bacteria, germs, and viruses.
188. I outgrow any childhood illnesses or inherited genetic disorders
189. I speak order to the chaos in any part of my body
190. My body is youthful, and time does not influence this fact
191. My health is always going to be remain stable

CHAPTER FOUR

POSITIVE AFFIRMATIONS FOR FINANCES

1. Money comes to me easily and effortlessly.
2. I constantly attract opportunities that create more money.
3. I am worthy of making more money.
4. I am open and receptive to all the wealth life offers me.
5. My actions create constant prosperity.
6. Money and spirituality co-exist harmoniously in my life
7. I attract money effortlessly and easily.
8. I continuously discover new avenues of income.
9. I am open to all the wealth life has to offer.
10. I use money to better other people's lives.
11. I attract lucrative opportunities to create money.
12. I see abundance everywhere.
13. I am becoming more and more prosperous with every day.
14. Life takes care of all my needs.
15. My life is full of prosperity.
16. I deserve abundance and prosperity.
17. Money spent comes back to me multiplied.
18. I have all the power I need to create the success I desire.
19. The universe provides bountiful opportunities for my success.
20. I refuse to be distracted from my goals and vision.
21. Every day is filled with new ideas and new possibilities.
22. Being successful comes easily to me.
23. I am worthy of financial stability.
24. I am open-minded and willing to explore any path to success.
25. Limiting beliefs have no power over me. I am optimistic and open-minded.

26. I expect to be successful in all of my endeavors. Success is my natural state.
27. I easily find solutions to challenges and roadblocks and move past them quickly.
28. Mistakes and setbacks are stepping stones to my success because I learn from them.
29. Every day in every way, I am becoming more and more successful.
30. I feel successful in my life right now, even as I work toward future success.
31. I know exactly what I need to do to achieve success.
32. I see fear as the fuel for my success and take bold action in spite of fear.
33. I feel powerful, capable, confident, energetic, and on top of the world.
34. I have an intention for success and know it is a reality awaiting my arrival.
35. I have now reached my goal and feel the excitement of my achievement.
36. I am attaining my financial goals from a place of contentment
37. Money comes to me effortlessly
38. I am a powerful money house
39. I do not owe people as I always fulfill my debts
40. I have all the resources I need to fulfill my financial obligations
41. I do not work for money. Money works for me
42. I have the intellectual resources to create wealth
43. I have the wisdom to make smart decisions about money
44. I enjoy the wealth that comes to me
45. Money is not a problem for me
46. I am a money magnet
47. I come up with innovative ideas that build wealth
48. I am a wealth creator
49. My actions are not governed by greed

50. As I apply myself in the pursuit of wealth, I do so legally
51. I have the right connections to get me to my financial goals
52. I control a conglomerate of wealth
53. My wealth is inexhaustible
54. I am able to provide for my family even on to the fifth generation
55. I break every limitation over my attaining wealth
56. I am prosperous in all of my endeavors
57. I am rich in every currency of the world
58. Poverty is far away from me
59. As I accumulate wealth, I am generous to the people around me
60. The works of my hands are blessed to consistently produce fruits
61. I eat the fruit of my labors
62. I am wealthy
63. I am rich
64. I am surrounded by abundance everywhere I go
65. There is no such thing as lack for me
66. I have the ability to buy everything I want
67. I am not foolish in the matters of wealth
68. I am plugged in to the source of wealth in the universe
69. All the elements I need to create and sustain wealth are available to me
70. Money is attracted to my endeavors
71. My wallet and bank accounts are never empty
72. I shall never be financially stranded
73. I have a positive attitude towards money
74. I breathe, eat and sleep in wealth
75. I have grossly exceeded my financial expectations this year
76. I am not a stranger to wealth
77. I break any hold that poverty has over my family
78. I develop money habits
79. I am making money throughout the day

80. I am making money when I am asleep and when I am awake
81. I have the foresight to anticipate potential money-making moves
82. I am well versed on the art of creating wealth
83. The wealth that I create is sustainable
84. The doors of opportunities that lead to wealth creation are open to me
85. Money for me is as abundant as the air that I breathe
86. I can never be poor in this life
87. I can never be broke in the life
88. I reject the seeds of poverty in my life
89. I surround myself with wealth creators
90. I am relating with some of the world's biggest financial influencers
91. I do not inherit the debt of my father and his father before him
92. I am financially equipped to meet the needs of my family
93. I am setting smart financial goals this year
94. The margin for failure in my life is next to none
95. I dwell in riches and wealth
96. I am an epitome of success and financial wealth
97. I enjoy my wealth
98. I am unfazed by the economic climate of the present times
99. My wealth is independent of what is going on in the world today
100. I make wise investment decisions
101. I make money moves that bring in rich dividends
102. I am a partaker in the divine wealth of the universe
103. I have been programmed for success
104. There is no such thing as limitation when it comes to making money
105. I speak the language of wealth creation fluently
106. The money in my account is abundant
107. At any point in time, I have the right resources to make a profitable transaction

108. I can never be poor in my life
109. I have an aversion to poverty
110. I think rich and wealthy thoughts
111. I am success on the move
112. Things don't happen to me in the world of finance, I happen to things
113. I am the boss of money, I tell money what to do
114. I am consistently creating wealth
115. I am dogged in my determination to remain wealthy
116. I am not appalled by wealth
117. I rule over money in my life
118. Success is not in the quote that I hang up on my wall, it is my experience
119. I walk in financial freedom daily
120. I am making good financial transactions everyday
121. My desire for wealth is not motivated by greed
122. I do not engage in any unlawful activity to build my wealth
123. The wealth that I possess is borne from intense hard work
124. I can never work in vain
125. Success and wealth are the rewards for my efforts
126. Wealth is a constant companion in my life
127. Being wealthy is my fundamental right and divine heritage
128. I am constantly making progress
129. Every minute of my day brings in wealth for me
130. My life is characterized by financial abundance
131. I am not ashamed of creating wealth
132. Any religious programming that shames me for being wealthy is deactivated
133. I was born to reign triumphantly in this life
134. I was created to be wealthy
135. I will not be defeated or defined by failed endeavors
136. The lessons that I learn in life empower me to be greater
137. I always win financially

138. My wealth is not just for display. I use it to actively transform my community positively
139. My wealth is protected from financial locusts
140. Because I am connected to the universal source of wealth, I can never run dry
141. Even in abundance, I know how to spend money wisely
142. My journey to greater success and wealth begins today
143. My financial expectations are not cut off
144. I am forging bonds with the right people to bring about the manifestation of my financial goals
145. I have total peace of mind concerning wealth
146. This is very little that I cannot accomplish financially
147. I have allies in the right places
148. Wealth is not a foreign concept to me
149. I am not defined by wealth, but my life is characterized by it
150. My mind is constantly working on innovative ways to create wealth
151. I move on own timeline for wealth actualization
152. I do not compare my financial journey to others
153. I will arrive at my financial destination on time regardless of circumstances
154. My journey to wealth is filled with excitement and joy
155. As I work towards my success goals, I release myself from worry and trepidation
156. I have access to treasures in hidden places
157. The knowledge of the hidden wealth of this world is mine
158. I have obtained divine favor to succeed in my financial endeavors
159. The creation of wealth is an effortless process for me
160. I excel in everything that I do
161. My wealth is like the leaves of an evergreen tree; it is renewed with each season and it never runs dry
162. I am divinely ordained to be a successful wealth creator

163. The economic policies of the world are working in my favor
164. Even when the world is in a season of loss, I am creating wealth
165. There nothing that is adequately equipped to stop me from being successful in life
166. Even I cannot sabotage my efforts to be successful
167. I am swimming in oceans of wealth
168. My financial motivations are not rooted in fear or greed
169. My biggest failure in life is not enough to stop me from prospering
170. Just like the phoenix, the ashes of my failure is a launch pad for my success
171. I am elevated above poverty
172. I am ridding myself of any poverty mentality that is holding me back from making progress in life
173. If I am sabotaging my own success with my hands, I am making the choice right now to put a stop to it
174. Money has a name and it responds to me when I call it
175. My wealth causes me to be a financial blessing to my world and the people in it
176. I elevate people with my wealth as I am not selfish
177. I feed myself with thoughts that motivate and excite the wealth creator in me
178. The wealth that I possess is not limited or restricted by any border
179. I am equipped to enjoy the wealth that I have created
180. I have the mindset of a wealth creator
181. My financial situation can never be hopeless
182. My mind is a wealth of ideas that I consistently mine for productive results
183. It is impossible for me to run out of money because the source of my wealth is within. As long as I am alive, I am making money

184. My financial future is consistently in an upward drive
185. I experience a consistent progression in the wealth that I create annually
186. I was borne to live a life of success
187. Every day, I am climbing from one level of success to another
188. I do not stand in the way of the successes of other people
189. I have a clear vision of the life that I want
190. I pursue my financial goals with renewed vigor each day
191. Today I am successful. Tomorrow I will be successful. Every day I am successful

CHAPTER FIVE

POSITIVE AFFIRMATIONS FOR BUSINESS

1. I am running one of the most successful businesses in the world
2. I easily accomplish all my business goals.
3. I only desire things that are in line with my business goals
4. I instantly manifest my desires.
5. The business that I run is not just making money. It is making a difference
6. I can achieve whatever I desire.
7. I can conquer all the challenges I am confronted with.
8. I am becoming more confident and stronger each day in the choices I make.
9. My potential to succeed is infinite.
10. In this business, I am becoming more knowledgeable and wiser with each day.
11. I am creative and bursting with brilliant ideas.
12. I am courageous and overcome my fears by confronting them.
13. Challenges bring out the best in me.
14. I have confidence in my abilities and skills.
15. I make sound financial decisions.
16. I am bold and courageous in pursuing my business goals.
17. I face difficulties associated with running a business with courage.
18. My business makes a profound difference in this world.
19. I am building a successful business for global impact.
20. I create value with my service. My business is a gift to this world.
21. I am savvy about business.

22. Each failure has made me a better businessman/businesswoman.
23. I am successful in whatever I do.
24. Failure teaches me how I can become successful in life.
25. I leave no stone unturned in my journey to become successful.
26. I attract divine success.
27. I am pursuing my own definition of success
28. Everything will work out for me.
29. I am a winner.
30. The tools I need to succeed are in my possession.
31. There is nobody better to get the job done than me.
32. I have faith in my business ideas
33. I am grateful for the things I have.
34. I will achieve all of my goals.
35. My goals are simple and uncomplicated
36. Clients will flock to me from different parts of the world
37. My goals are getting closer to completion every day.
38. I set clear goals and work to complete them every day.
39. I have a plan of action to achieve my desires.
40. My priorities are clear. I work to finish my most important tasks first.
41. My goals are my focus.
42. I only set goals that matter.
43. My focus on success is unwavering
44. When my need is strong enough, I will find a way.
45. I am committed to becoming the person I will become.
46. My mind is like water. I will change and adjust as needed in business.
47. Success is in the future of my business
48. I will master distractions and keep my focus on my goals.
49. I must rely upon myself.
50. Blame for failure rests upon my shoulders but it would not hold me down.

51. I am my own best chance for success.
52. I will accept nothing but the best.
53. Success is in my future.
54. I am constantly improving.
55. I desire to learn new things.
56. Where others see a challenge, I see new opportunities.
57. I have a growth mindset.
58. Time is my friend. I finish all the tasks I need to finish.
59. My life is made for joy. I will build my business with exuberance.
60. I will be proactive in discovering obstacles to my accomplishments.
61. Mindfulness will help me get the most from my time.
62. I take responsibility for my successes and my failures.
63. I am not dependent on anyone else.
64. I follow my dreams with vigor.
65. The little things in life make all the difference.
66. I enjoy being surrounded by the people I work with
67. My fear diminishes as I live my life with courage.
68. A successful business man/woman lives within me, and today that woman/man is running my business.
69. I am confident and calm.
70. Doors of opportunity and abundance open to me today.
71. New opportunities come easily to me.
72. There are no limits to what I can achieve.
73. Today I am optimistic. I think positively and surround myself with positive energy.
74. I feel strong, excited, and powerful about the future of my business.
75. I regularly add income to my business.
76. Today I will move my business forward.
77. Amazing opportunities are constantly coming my way.
78. I attract positive customers and team members to my business.

79. There are no limits to what I can and will achieve today.
80. I can and I will do this! There is nothing stopping me.
81. I will work smarter, not harder.
82. I am a positive influence, and I surround myself with others like me.
83. Time is my most valuable asset. I guard my time carefully.
84. Balance is key. I will mix self-care with effort.
85. My progress is always moving forward.
86. I feel free to give myself the TLC I need.
87. Positive energy surrounds me.
88. I am a wonderful employer. My employees are lucky to have me.
89. My business goals will manifest as just as it is in my dreams.
90. When I say "no" to the wrong project, I move that much closer to the peace of mind I need in business and I understand this.
91. My new business income will continue to increase.
92. I am calm and confident in running the affairs of my business.
93. New opportunities come easily to me.
94. I will attract positive customers.
95. When business opportunities knock, I am more than prepared to answer the door.
96. Organization comes naturally to me.
97. I control my day; I will not let my day control me.
98. My passion for business brings tangible results.
99. I will not let others impose their limitations on me.
100. I am fully committed to achieving success in my life.
101. My only limit is myself.
102. My intuition and wisdom guide me in the right direction.
103. I have faith in myself.
104. I am able to meet the best decision possible for my business daily
105. I have confidence in my decisions as I intuitively know what is right for business

106. Even if I meet the wrong decision, it will always lead me somewhere positive.
107. I make responsible business decisions and consider how they affect other people.
108. . I reach any business goal I set my mind to. If I dream it, I can do it. No goal is out of reach.
109. I never stop learning and see opportunities for growth everywhere. I improve every day for the rest of my life.
110. My business today is better than it was at this point last year, and it is becoming better and better with each passing day.
111. I am programmed to hire the right kind of people in my business
112. I am patient with myself as I pursue my business goals and accept that positive changes may take some time. But different elements of my vision for my business is emerging every day.
113. My employees are passionate about the positive outcome of my business just as I am
114. I release my attachment to anything that does not serve me in pursuant of my business goals. I don't let anything, or anybody hold me back. I am finished with negativity in my life.
115. I have found a way to effectively communicate my business ideas to the people would assist me in making it a reality
116. I ask for what I want because I deserve it. I honor my desires today and always.
117. I do not fear for the future of my business as I have successfully mapped out the pathway to success and I have mitigated any possible threat to the success of that business
118. Regardless of any situation that confronts me, I am blessed. I am blessed with every lesson I learn from hardships

I face. I continue to grow in light of all of the positive and negative things that come my way.
119. I am consciously making the effort to remain excited about business
120. I reach my goals even if I make mistakes because I know there is nothing to stop me from getting what I want.
121. If I reach a point where I am struggling with growth in business, I get divine inspiration on how to take things to the next level
122. I do not allow other people to hold me back from achieving my goals. I give myself permission to walk my own path and allow other people to do the same.
123. I am built to handle the success capacity of my business so that I do not get overwhelmed by it at any point
124. The success capacity of my business exceeds my personal expectations and the projection of others
125. I forgive the people who have hurt me in business to release myself from any past pain. As I forgive, I experience freedom. I am leaving the past errors in the past, and I am only living for the present and the future.
126. I know what I want, and I know I deserve it. I take responsibility for everything I have brought into my business.
127. My business motivation comes from a place of peace
128. I am hungry to drive the vision that I have for my business forward
129. I am not hesitant execute the brilliant business strategies that I have
130. The road to my success is exciting and full of delight
131. I find fulfillment in the success of my business
132. My business is able to satisfy the needs of my clients
133. I am building sustainable solutions with my business
134. My business is the answer to the needs of my client
135. At any point in time, the word "no" does not define the outcome of my business

136. I get more yeses than no
137. People may try to copy my business but the uniqueness of my business model and ideas make my business to stand out
138. I make fair and rational decisions in business
139. My business competes favorably in the global market
140. I am awarded contracts that positively impacts my business
141. Every job assigned to my company is an opportunity to shine and I am always eager to execute them
142. I do not take anything that happens to me in business for granted
143. My company is an exciting place for employees to work in
144. The best hands in the business are always eager to come and work for me
145. The team spirit in my company is such that we feel like a family unit
146. I have created a conducive work atmosphere for both clients and workers
147. Every negative and disruptive force is repelled from me or my business today
148. I have the right kind of attitude towards a successful business
149. I have all the resources need to take my business from where it is right now to where I would like it to be tomorrow
150. There are no restrictions or limitations to the kind of success that my business attains
151. My business is an extension of my dreams and through it, I am able to achieve the other dreams that I have
152. The atmosphere above, around and within my business is positive
153. My business is always relevant
154. The business that I build is a legacy that will be inherited by the generations to come
155. I am moving forward, and the success of this business is in an upward projectile

156. My business is success in motion
157. The foundations I have laid for this business is strong enough to enable it weather whatever economic climate it finds itself in
158. I am attracting the right kind of investors for my business
159. I leave nothing to chance in the affairs of my business
160. I find favor and grace in all of my business dealings
161. I have a strong and supporting base and this gives me confidence
162. I do not lose sight of my goals or objectives at any point
163. I am daily inspired to be excellent
164. I refuse to operate my business at the level of mediocrity
165. I employ sound business principles that deliver profitable results
166. My business world is on a global stage and I thrive in it
167. I am employing the right kind of talent needed for my business to take it to the next level
168. My business net worth is vastly impacted by my network as I am making the right kind of connections
169. I never fail in business as I am always winning or learning. The failures that come as lessons are my launch pad for greater things
170. The future for my business is bright. All dark clouds have dissipated
171. I do not run my business on debt. I am sufficiently able to keep my investors happy
172. As I make good financial decisions, I am also making sound social, political and environmental choices
173. I am able to run my business and still lead a life that is fun and fulfilling
174. The contracts that I sign in my business are in my favor
175. My business is protected against the vices of economic devourers that have led to the sudden demise of many businesses

176. Money is not the main objective of my business. I am dominating in my field
177. There is no challenge that is insurmountable for me in business
178. I have the right people in my corner, so my business is in the right hands
179. My business advisers have my best interest at heart
180. I do not lose money to theft, carelessness or by accidents
181. In the case of an accident, I have the wisdom to put the right steps in place to mitigate against such
182. There is order and thorough organization in my business
183. My business is a source of joy to me and many people
184. Through me and my business, the lives of many people have been impacted positively
185. I am breaking the mold and creating new pathways in business
186. My business stands out as a shining example of how businesses should be done
187. My business is winning global awards in different fronts for excellence
188. My business is associated with quality, superiority, excellence and innovation
189. I have a very happy customer base
190. Through my business, I am meeting with world leaders and global influencers
191. I am made to run a successful business and this business is going to e a lasting legacy that will stand the test of time.
192. There is nothing stopping me from growing. I seize opportunities and make things happen.

CHAPTER SIX

POSITIVE AFFIRMATIONS FOR CONFIDENCE

1. I remember myself as the master that I am, the master I have always been.
2. I know I have mastery over my life by how still I can keep my mind and how alert I am in the now.
3. I use my power lovingly when I have influence over others
4. I am connected to divine love and wisdom.
5. I am clear, untainted, and unharmed by any negative that I have experienced in my life.
6. I trust in the process of life
7. My possibilities are endless.
8. I am worthy of my dreams.
9. I am enough.
10. It is easy for me to look in the mirror and say, "I love you."
11. I am attractive.
12. My partner finds my sexy because (he/she) is attracted to every part of me.
13. I love everything about my body.
14. I radiate confidence and others respect me.
15. Others find me sexy and desirable.
16. I am filled with excitement when I look in the mirror.
17. I am rewarded for doing my best.
18. Every action I take increases my confidence.
19. I see problems as interesting challenges.
20. I radiate confidence.
21. I am worthy of happiness and love.

22. I feel relaxed and comfortable around other people.
23. I enjoy meeting new people. I even seek out others.
24. I am outgoing. I can enrich other people's lives.
25. I am easy to talk to. I am confident when I am around others
26. I get better with each day. Practice helps me to attain greatness.
27. I believe in my ability to overcome drawbacks.
28. I replace every unconstructive criticism with encouraging support.
29. Perfection can be found in all my flaws.
30. I always give my best and am a good-hearted person.
31. Other people will not take advantage of me.
32. I have confidence in my skills.
33. I am not afraid to be wrong.
34. Happiness is within my grasp.
35. I am confident in the presence of others.
36. Success will be my driving force.
37. The success of others will not make me jealous. My time will come.
38. I will speak with confidence and self-assurance.
39. I will say "No" when I do not have the time or inclination to act.
40. The only person who can defeat me is myself.
41. I dare to be different.
42. My every desire is achievable.
43. Even outside my comfort zone, I will be comfortable in my own skin.
44. If I fail, I will fail forward.
45. My confidence knows no limits.
46. I do not need other people for happiness.
47. I choose hope over fear.
48. Positivity is a choice that I choose to make.
49. I will not take another person's negativity personally.
50. My commitment to myself is real

51. I believe in me.
52. I acknowledge my self-worth–my confidence is soaring.
53. I am not my mistakes.
54. I accept myself unconditionally.
55. I am proud of myself and all that I have accomplished.
56. I am successful.
57. I am a beautiful person.
58. I deserve love, compassion, and empathy.
59. I believe in the person I dream of becoming.
60. I choose to be happy and completely love myself today.
61. I honor my commitments to myself.
62. There is no wrong decision.
63. I am now creating my life exactly as I want it.
64. Positivity is a choice; I choose to be positive.
65. I am free of worry and am at peace with who I am.
66. I matter. I am allowed to say "no" to others and "yes to myself.
67. What I give is what I receive.
68. I choose not to take it personally.
69. I will stop apologizing for being myself.
70. Negative self-talk has no place in my life.
71. I do not bow to my fears.
72. My mind, body, and soul are fit and strong.
73. When I breathe, I inhale confidence and exhale timidity.
74. I love meeting strangers and approach them with boldness and enthusiasm.
75. I live in the present and am confident of the future.
76. My personality exudes confidence. I am bold and outgoing.
77. I am self-reliant, creative and persistent in whatever I do.
78. I am energetic and enthusiastic. Confidence is my second nature.
79. I always attract only the best of circumstances and the best positive people in my life.

80. I am a problem solver. I focus on solutions and always find the best solution.
81. I love change and easily adjust myself to new situations.
82. I am well groomed, healthy and full of confidence. My outer self is matched by my inner well-being.
83. Self-confidence is what I thrive on. Nothing is impossible and life is great.
84. I face difficult situations with courage and conviction. I always find a way out of such situations.
85. I always see only the good in others. I attract only positive confident people
86. I use my emotions, thoughts and challenges to lead me to deeper, more interesting places within myself.
87. I am grateful for all that I am
88. I am grateful to be alive. It is my joy and pleasure to live another wonderful day.
89. Happiness is my birth right. I choose to be happy and I deserve to be happy.
90. Being happy comes easy to me. Happiness is my second nature.
91. I am deeply fulfilled by what I do.
92. I love my face and all my features and see my imperfections as signs of a life well-lived.
93. I am a source of knowledge that people seek out when they need information.
94. I am constantly amazed by my body and its abilities.
95. I exude confidence when I go out in the world and others see it in me.
96. I hold my head up high and put a smile on my face every day.
97. I let go of my need to impress other people. There is nothing that I need to prove. I accept myself just as I am.
98. I am excited to show the world who I am and everything I have to offer. No one can stop me from meeting my goals.

99. I am brave and willing to embrace my full power. I have complete control over my actions and my life.
100. I am the president of my life and no one else can take that role. I trust myself to make the best decisions for my life.
101. I have infinite possibilities today. I love life and I am ready to take inspired and motivated action on my goals.
102. I don't have to wait until I feel ready to act on my goals. The timing will never be right. I'm ready now.
103. I will take action despite any fear of failure. No matter what, I am proud of myself for trying.
104. I am not afraid of the unknown because I know I can overcome all the challenges that come my way.
105. I embrace my full potential, even if it makes other people uncomfortable. I do not play small. I am supposed to do big things.
106. I radiate respect and love and I get it in return.
107. I am enough. Always.
108. I am love.
109. I am loving.
110. I am loved.
111. I trust in the person I am.
112. I am kind to myself.
113. I make time to look after myself.
114. I deserve love and respect.
115. I am strong and capable.
116. I have a lot to offer the world.
117. I am sunshine.
118. I have a beautiful laugh.
119. My smile makes others smile.
120. I exude warmth and kindness.
121. My heart is full of love for who I am.
122. Love is what I believe in most of all.
123. My hugs are full of love and warmth.
124. I bring joy to the world.

125. I rock at being me!
126. I am proud of the person I am today, and the person I will be tomorrow.
127. I work hard and know my worth.
128. I have many skills to offer.
129. I place value on the experience I have, and my ability to learn and grow more.
130. I have the inner strength to navigate challenges at work.
131. I have my own definition of success.
132. I take pride in the work I do.
133. Work is an important part of my life but it is not my sole purpose or passion.
134. When I work, I apply myself with focus and positivity.
135. I take time to rest after working hard.
136. I am reliable, responsible and respected at work.
137. I am a creative person.
138. There is always a place in the world for my creativity.
139. I share what I create with pride and grace.
140. The world wants more of what I have to offer.
141. There is always a place in the world for what I create and make.
142. I am passionate about my creativity.
143. My creativity has a purpose in my life and in the world.
144. My life is fuller when I make time and space for my creativity.
145. I keep my eyes, ears and heart open for creative inspiration.
146. I focus on what I can control, and I let go of what I can't.
147. I love my beautiful mind.
148. I invest in myself through big and small acts of self-care and self-love.
149. My inner strength knows no bounds.
150. I breathe in energy and love, I exhale negativity and doubt.
151. I take time to know my needs, limits and boundaries better.

152. I know that good mental health is a journey, not a destination.
153. My mental health is just as important as my physical health.
154. I'm not ashamed or alone in having mental health struggles.
155. I look after my mental health because it deserves my love.
156. I am always stronger than I look and feel.
157. The joy that I feel today resonates throughout my body
158. I am full of positive energy
159. I am in a safe space mentally, emotionally and physically
160. I recognise the divinity that lives within me and I pay homage to my greatness
161. I have a winning mentality in everything that I apply myself to do
162. I am strong. I cannot be crippled by my circumstances
163. My mind is a safe haven for all my insecurities
164. I am perfect in all my imperfections
165. My failures or mistakes do not define my personality. I am a winner
166. I am a success going into the world to happen
167. I am a person of excellence. I do not deal in mediocrity
168. I have overcome the hurdles of today to become better than I was yesterday
169. I rise above challenges and limiting circumstances
170. I have defeated the traumas of my past and I am no longer defined by my history
171. I am getting better in every way
172. My strengths have compensated for my weaknesses and I am better for it
173. Today, I choose to be a victor and not a victim
174. I have been emotionally and mentally programmed to be a success. Nothing can stand in my way

175. I will not be intimidated by the circumstances or challenges in my life
176. This is my appointed time for greatness and I will rise to the occasion
177. Today I have the courage to advocate for my peace and happiness
178. I refuse to be bullied or silenced into accepting situations that are not good for me
179. I have the courage to prioritize my needs and wants above others
180. I am not a selfish person but I do not think less of myself either
181. I engage in activities that promote my happiness and joy
182. I will not sabotage my own happiness today because I am aware and I believe that I deserve it
183. The only person I am in a competition with is myself and i strive to be better
184. Because I am aware of my self-worth, I refuse to give up on myself
185. I have a sound mind and I am making strategic decisions that will work in my favour
186. I am not afraid to fail that because I am aware that failure cannot hold me down
187. I am not ordinary. I am an extraordinary human being
188. I am not afraid to take calculated risks because I am bold
189. I am bold. I am gold and I am exceptionally blessed
190. I walk tall and am proud of who I am.
191. I am the author of my own story, therefore, I do not live according to the script of other people. I am the leading character in my life

CHAPTER SEVEN

POSITIVE AFFIRMATIONS FOR PEACE OF MIND

1. I am at peace.
2. As I become more and more aware of myself as eternal consciousness, I become more peaceful and at ease with all that happens in my life.
3. Physical reality reflects this peace back to me.
4. My relationships are loving and harmonious
5. I am a channel for loving peaceful energy
6. I am harmonious and at peace regardless of my surroundings
7. My body is relaxed. My soul is at peace. My mind is calm
8. My intuition and inner wisdom guide me in every situation
9. Life always wants the best for me.
10. The challenges I'm confronted with are opportunities for growth.
11. Every time I exhale, I breathe out tensions and anxieties.
12. Every situation serves my highest good.
13. I am calm, patient, and in control of my emotions.
14. The more I give, the more I will receive.
15. My negative thoughts and self-images are gone.
16. My strength is stronger than my anxiety.
17. I move beyond stress to peace.
18. My thoughts are positive and full of joy.
19. I am safe. I trust life, and I trust in myself.
20. I feel wonderfully peaceful and relaxed.
21. I let go of everything that worries me. I will confront these challenges tomorrow.
22. My mind is at peace.

23. My world is a peaceful, loving, and joy-filled place to live.
24. I sow the seeds of peace wherever I go.
25. I surround myself with peaceful people.
26. My work environment is calm and peaceful.
27. I breathe in peace, I breathe out chaos and disorder.
28. My home is a peaceful sanctuary where I feel safe and happy.
29. In all that I say and do, I choose peace.
30. I release past anger and hurts and fill myself with serenity and peaceful thoughts.
31. Peace descends all around me now and always.
32. I send peace from myself into the world.
33. I respond peacefully in all situations.
34. I am grounded in the experience of the present moment.
35. I am focused and engaged in the task at hand.
36. I am conscious that all is well right now.
37. I am grateful for this moment and find joy in it.
38. I am free of anxiety, and a calm inner peace fills my mind and body.
39. I am not my thoughts and pay attention to my actions without judging them.
40. I am fully present in all of my relationships.
41. I am unique. I feel good about being alive and being me.
42. I find deep inner peace within myself as I am.
43. I am completely pain-free, and my body is full of energy.
44. Every day I am more and more at ease.
45. I am in the present moment and release the past to live fully now
46. I have a peaceful aura around me and I influences those around me
47. Calmness washes over me with every deep breath I take.
48. I meditate easily without resistance or anxiety.
49. Being calm and relaxed energizes my whole being.
50. All the muscles in my body are releasing and relaxing.

51. All negativity and stress are evaporating from my body and my mind.
52. I breathe in relaxation. I breathe out stress.
53. Even when there is chaos around me, I remain calm and centered.
54. I transcend stress of any kind. I live in peace.
55. I gently and easily return to the present moment.
56. All is well in my world. I am calm, happy, and content.
57. I fall into a deep and relaxing sleep.
58. I am deliberate in my pursuit of peace
59. Every encounter or interaction with me can be described as peaceful
60. I actively pursue peace with myself as well as peace with the people around me
61. I engage in activities that bring about a peaceful and clear state of mind
62. I have made peace with mistakes I made in the last. I refused to be consumed by guilt for those actions
63. I take out time throughout the day to cultivate thoughts and words that promote the peace of my mind
64. I cancel out any negative vibes that threatens the piece of my mind
65. I have found my happy space and I guard it zealously
66. I feel blessed to live the life that I live today
67. I stay in the moment and I am not worried or anxious about what will happen tomorrow
68. I release myself from any negative emotion that is stressing me out
69. Even in the eye of the storm I remain calm
70. I am as grounded as the Earth therefore I remain unshakeable in the face of trials
71. I understand that life is a cycle of ups and downs. I may be down today but there is definitely an up tomorrow and I am calm in this knowledge

72. I am rooted in the reality of the knowledge that this too will pass
73. My mind is like a slow running brook on a sunny day. It is clear, clean and calm
74. My body reacts positively to stress.
75. I recognize the stressors in my environment and I wisely avoid them
76. I surround myself with people who are interested in keeping the peace
77. I have the mental foresight to plan ahead and save myself from unnecessary stress
78. I am an embodiment of calm and rational living
79. I am not troubled by the expectations of other people
80. I do not wallow in fear of what might or might not happen tomorrow
81. I have the courage to accept the things that I cannot change in my life
82. I have successfully created an atmosphere that is calm amd serene every where I go
83. Situations that usually stirred panic and anxiety have lost their hold over me
84. I distance myself from people who are bent on robbing me of my peace
85. The peace that I experience daily is not a fickle thing. It is as solid as a rock
86. Today, I choose to experience peace
87. I am a conduit for peace and harmony in my world
88. I acknowledge and accept my responsibility as a peacemaker
89. I make the effort to ensure that in all my relationships, peace is maintained
90. The decisions I am taking in my life today bring peace to my mind and my soul
91. I rise above the trials in my life that cause me to be anxious and take solace in the joy that is promised tomorrow

92. When trouble arises I am not swallowed up in panic
93. My actions are not motivated by fear. Rather I come from a place of clear thinking
94. I have a sound mind. I refuse to be afraid
95. The events in my life today would release an outpouring of peace and serenity
96. The universe is collaborating with every positive force in my life to ensure that my peace of mind is retained
97. I am aware of the benefits of dwelling in this place of serenity and I do everything within my power to protect it
98. The events of this day cannot compromise the peace that I know
99. Peace flows into my life today like an endless stream of water
100. I have a clear sound mind
101. I am at peace with everyone including people who consider themselves my enemies
102. The peace that I experience is rooted in sources beyond my circumstances
103. I am able to recognize healthy relationships in my life through the peace of mind that I experience in them
104. I surround my heart and my mind with a hedge that protects it from negative thoughts or emotions
105. I am consistent in participating in practices that promote my peace of mind
106. Today, I refuse to be anxious
107. Everyday, I am making the choice to consciously engage in emotions that are more productive than worry and anxiety
108. Today, I refuse to worry about things that I have absolutely no control over
109. I am replacing the burdens of my fears with the consistent flow of peace into my life
110. I do not dwell on the fears of tomorrow but rather, I live in the joy of the moment

111. I am making a conscious effort not to postpone my happiness because of fears and worries
112. I speak peace into my day
113. I am an ambassador for peace
114. I have learned to avoid situations that rob me of my peace
115. Every breath that I take draws in peace and restores serenity of mind while every breath that I release lets go of every feeling of fear and anxiety
116. As I control my breathing, I am able to control any emotion that stirs up panic and anxiety inside of me
117. I am well-versed in practices, affirmations and actions that calm me in the event of a panic attack
118. My mind is a healthy place that is rich in peace and happiness
119. I have all the resources I need to create a peaceful ambiance and atmosphere in my home
120. My home is imbued with so much peace and serenity that people forget their troubles the moment they step inside it
121. I have overcome my fears and found solace in the voice within
122. Even when darkness comes I am able to find peace
123. The pains and anxieties I have struggled with in the past no longer control my state of mind
124. I plug the peace of mind that I enjoy today into the universal source of peace
125. My mind is not like a ship that is beaten and tossed about on the sea with every wave or tempest that comes. Instead, I stand like a mountain...unwavering and unshaken
126. The peace of mind that I experience is genuine
127. The affairs of life cannot stop me from experiencing happiness
128. My happiness and peace go hand-in-hand as I do not experience one without experiencing the other

129. I have chosen this day to own my peace of mind because I deserve to be happy
130. There is so much peace and happiness embedded within that I do not need to look outside for happiness
131. I am no longer disappointed by the actions of other people as I have chosen to place a higher value on my happiness and where it comes from
132. My life is a constant parade of joy, happiness, peace and wellness and I am at the centre of it all
133. I do not live my life in regrets. I have made the decisions I have made, and taken the actions I have taken. And today, I have made peace with all of them
134. I am taking the deliberate step to sow seeds today that will yield profitable returns in my future tomorrow giving me a platform to rid myself of anxiety
135. The peace and calmness that I experience is contagious. People who come in contact with me immediately reflect the calmness that I feel
136. I have a vivid vision of the future that I desire, therefore, even dark circumstances cannot shake me
137. I know my place in the universe and I have come to a place of acceptance of it
138. I have a very good understanding of my purpose in life so I am not anxious about it
139. I am not afraid of the challenges that lie ahead
140. I know that I have a triumphant victory awaiting me so, even this present failure cannot hold me down
141. I am wise enough to know that giving into my fears is coming into acceptance of a possible outcome that is yet to be determined
142. Today, I am choosing to accept the possibility that all will be well with me

143. I have successfully trained the lions that prowl in my nightmares and successfully converted my fears into a podium for triumph
144. Worrying is pointless so I have chosen to not waste my time on it
145. I am a peaceful force to be reckoned with nothing can hold me down
146. I am calm and serene in the face of troubles
147. I am capable of consistently making rational decisions because I do not operate from a place of chaos
148. I am a reliable, capable and strong partner in a time of crisis because I am always calm
149. I am capable of sieving through the rubble in order to make a clear and concise decision
150. My life right now is a constant manifestation of peace and happiness
151. Even in the darkest night, I am able to see the light at the end of the tunnel
152. I let go of anxiety and embrace calmness
153. I let go of fear and embrace courage
154. I let go of worry and embrace confidence
155. I let go of panic and embrace stillness
156. I let go of chaos and embrace order
157. I let go of pain and embrace healing
158. I let go of grief and embrace the blessed memories
159. I let go of sadness and embrace joy
160. I let go of heartbreak and embrace love
161. I let go of guilt and embrace freedom
162. I let go of hatred and embrace acceptance
163. I let go of greed and embrace contentment
164. I let go of darkness and embrace the light
165. I let go of self-hate and embrace self-love
166. I let go of fakeness and embrace authenticity
167. I let go of expectations and embrace possibilities

168. I let go of losses and embrace recovery
169. I let go of past glory and embrace my future journeys
170. I let go of mistakes and embrace prospects
171. I let go of overindulgence and embrace moderation
172. I let go of jealousy and embrace trust
173. I let go of anger and embrace remorse
174. I let go of failures and embrace lessons
175. I let go of apprehension and embrace beautiful surprises
176. I let go of distractions and embrace things that interests me
177. I let go of aggression and embrace cohesion
178. I let go of pensiveness and embrace optimism
179. I let go of excuses and embrace accomplishments
180. I let go of bitter thoughts and embrace positive memories
181. I let go of shame and embrace my uniqueness
182. I let go of poor self-esteem and embrace the power within
183. I let go of disapproval and embrace my awesomeness
184. I let go of control and embrace fluidity
185. I let go of pride and embrace humility
186. I let go of confusion and embrace soundness of mind
187. I let go of criticisms and embrace self-affirmations
188. All I need to do right now is breathe
189. I am in a safe space and a warm, positive energy surrounds me
190. I let go of any burden that has affected my sleep
191. I go to bed knowing that all is well with my world.
192. I am at peace and feeling very sleepy. I am ready to fall asleep.

CHAPTER EIGHT

POSITIVE AFFIRMATIONS FOR SPIRITUALITY

1. The divine guides all my actions.
2. I am a spiritual being that is divinely guided.
3. I am in alignment with the universe.
4. God's grace and love is working through me.
5. I emanate love and joy, complete presence and openness, toward all beings.
6. All problems are illusions of the mind and I am enlightened enough to recognize this
7. I am a bring of light. I do not pollute my beautiful, radiant Inner Being, nor the Earth, with negativity. I do not give unhappiness, in any form, whatsoever, a dwelling place inside me.
8. My peace is so vast and so deep and rooted in the supernatural, that anything that is not peace, disappears into it, as if it had never existed.
9. I am spiritual enough to find creative express for myself.
10. No negative deed that was ever done to me, or which I did to others, can touch, even in the slightest way, the radiant essence of who I really am.
11. I am a Divine creation, a vital piece of God. Therefore, I cannot be undeserving.
12. I am empathetic and compassionate. I perceive the experiences of others just as acutely as I feel mine
13. Because I am spiritually attuned, I am powerful enough to overcome negativity.
14. I am connected to an unlimited source of abundance.

15. I have the ability to accomplish any task I set my mind to with ease and comfort.
16. My focus is not on the million things I may have to do at some future time, but on the one thing I can do right now
17. I have access to unlimited assistance. My strength comes from my connection to my Source of being.
18. I am content with what I have. I rejoice in the way things are because I have the spiritual foresight to know that everything I working out in my favor.
19. I relax and cast aside all of my burdens, allowing God to express through me His perfect love, peace, and wisdom.
20. I realize that there is nothing lacking. The whole world belongs to me.
21. God is within and around me, protecting me; so I will banish the fear that shuts out His guiding light.
22. I am an infinite being. The age of my body has no bearing on what I do or who I am.
23. The healing power of Spirit is flowing through all the cells of my body.
24. In all my cells, the healing light of God is shining. My cells are entirely well, for His perfection is in them.
25. God's perfect health permeates the dark nooks of my bodily sickness.
26. As I unclutter my life, I free myself to answer the callings of my soul.
27. Daily I will seek happiness more and more within my mind, and less and less through material pleasures.
28. I have infinite patience when it comes to fulfilling my destiny as ordained by God
29. I am constantly submerged in eternal light.
30. I live in the present moment by being grateful for all of my life experiences as a child.
31. I am made of the one universal God-substance.

32. Being myself as I was created involves no risks. It's my ultimate truth, and I live fearlessly in it
33. With the sword of devotion to the God I serve fervently, I sever all heart-strings that tie me to any delusions about my true essence
34. I will purify my mind empty myself of fear with the thought that God is guiding my every move.
35. The light of the Universe permeates every particle of my being.
36. I am with God and God is with me always.
37. With a deep and sincere love, I lay my heart at the feet of the Omnipresent one.
38. God's love is working through me now and always
39. I am an extension of God's love
40. I will always endeavor to help people who are weeping to smile, by smiling myself, even when it is difficult to do so.
41. The Divine Spirit is omnipresent. I fell it all around me and I am guided at every step of this journey called life
42. I am living in that light. The Divine Spirit fills me within and without
43. All my thoughts, words and actions are divinely guided.
44. God is the shepherd of my restless thoughts. He will lead them to His abode of peace.
45. The Universe naturally and freely provides for all my needs. So, I am unbothered.
46. I am strong in my faith and in my beliefs
47. I am a spiritual being having a human experience.
48. My mind and body are in complete alignment with the Universe and I am always in the flow.
49. My spirituality boldly expresses my faith in my God
50. My faith and beliefs are alive to me
51. I am responsible for my own spiritual growth.
52. I am bold in the knowledge of the divine power and love that is awake within me

53. I give gratitude to the divinity I have chosen to acknowledge
54. The words that feed my spiritual growth comes alive to me in all areas of my life
55. I trust that everything in my life is working for my highest good and I am receiving all that I am meant to have.
56. My faith and spirituality remain unshakable.
57. My faith in the divine keeps me humble
58. I am a divine expression of a loving God.
59. I give gratitude and praise to God in the highest
60. My life is characterized by an expression of God's divinity
61. I am grounded in the principles that guide my faith
I let go of fear. I let go of pain. I live in love.
62. I grow stronger and stronger in my faith everyday
63. My spirituality is drawn from a deep Faith in God and all things divine
64. My faith surrounds me and makes me whole
65. The people I encounter recognize my faith and are inspired by it
66. I am a loving, kind and forgiving person, in accordance with my spiritual nature.
67. My faith in God gives me courage and confidence.
68. I pay just as much attention to my spiritual health as I do my mental and physical health
69. I know that I can master anything, with divine guidance
70. I am guided by a force greater than myself
71. The love of God flows through me. I am His, He is mine.
72. The love of God radiate through me
73. God loves me completely and wholesomely
74. I am love personified
75. The universal plan for my life is full of love, peace and joy
76. My home is full of Gods love
77. I surrender to God. He is always with me. I do only his bidding.
78. I channel the energy and love of the infinite

79. I ask for forgiveness from all those whom I may have wronged and forgive all those who may have wronged me..
80. My faith in God lifts up those around me
81. My faith in a higher spirit keeps me grounded
82. Religion to me is a way of life. It is a way of living a morally and ethically correct life.
83. My Faith is the foundation of my Life and I live my Life according to my Faith in God
84. I am committed to God and naturally, God is committed to me too
85. I am surrounded by the love of God
86. My higher spirit guides me in the direction of my dreams.
87. When I love people more, I receive even more love from the universe in return.
88. My relationship with God is a powerful relationship
89. My faith in God sets me free from all worry, anxiety and doubt.
90. All is well
91. I let go and put my life in God's hands to guide and lead me
92. When my intentions are clear, the Universe cooperates with me and I can accomplish anything.
93. I think of only positive things and the universe ensures positive things happen in my life.
94. I feel a spiritual essence that is always with me, guiding me.
95. My faith lifts me above my fears
96. I am together with the Divine, here and now.
97. I breath in my spiritual vitality and feel alive everyday
98. I am aligned with my higher purpose.
99. I believe Gods path for me is abundant and joyous
100. All things are possible in the name of God, our father
101. I trust that all the events in my life are unfolding as they are meant to be.
102. As I abide in love for all creatures, they have cone to abide in love for me.

103. I love with the perfect Love of God. I see with the perfect eyes of God.
104. I respectfully ask for Divine guidance in all areas of my life.
105. The divine Spirit is now guiding my steps and all is unfolding for my good.
106. I am strong in my faith of a higher power
107. I am guided by the Universe and part of a bigger plan.
108. I create the perfect plan for my life by choosing the perfect thoughts.
109. My life experiences lead me to be closer to God. God knows what is the best possible gift for me at any moment.
110. I am a perfect, open channel for divine Peace, divine Love, divine Abundance, and divine Inspiration.
111. The entirety of creation is now conspiring for my good.
112. I am a winner and I attract only success through the power of my faith.
113. I am a magnet for the unlimited good things of God and I attract it effortlessly and easily.
114. I open my mind and heart to the perfect love of God.
115. I gratefully accept the totality and wholesomeness of all my good benefits
116. Today, as God opens the windows of heaven and pours me out a blessing, I make room to receive it.
117. The divine ruler of the universe gives me all that I want and need
118. I pursue an authentic relationship with God.
119. I know that my light shines because the Divine Light within me is always shining brightly.
120. I put my life in the hands of Infinite Love and Divine Wisdom.
121. The secrets of eternity are now revealed to me and they have become my reality

122. Infinite Love flows through me, in me, as me.
123. I am a manifestation of the divine presence
124. I am now attracting everything I need, effortlessly and easily.
125. My Faith makes me feel whole in spirit, soul and body.
126. Everything I seek is now seeking me.
127. I lift God up on high and he lifts me up
128. I am part of a spiritually enchanted world filled with exciting opportunities and ideas.
129. My every spiritual experience is filled with joy.
130. In every moment, I know exactly what to do and how to do it. I am spiritually wise and attuned
131. I embrace the glorious mess that my life may seem now, and offer it up as a prayer in gratitude.
132. My life belongs to God
133. I open the doors the lead to my good benefits and lay claim on my Divine inheritance.
134. Every cell in my body is now functioning in perfect Divine order.
135. The world around me is my playground, and I find joy in every experience.
136. I am proud to be part of nature. My world is filled with oceans of love and mountains of courage.
137. My faith and spiritual insight creates my reality
138. I have many strengths and talents inspired by nature. Nature helps me understand I am part of an infinite world with no end.
139. I am now enveloped by the Divine, embraced and cherished, nurtured and protected.
140. I am the expression of a loving God
141. The divine Spirit is around me, always.
142. I am perfect in the eyes of the divine.
143. I abide in the perfect wholeness of creation.
144. I am where the universe wants me to be.

145. I delight in the grace and mercy of God.
146. I am an eternal being with infinite possibilities surrounding me.
147. I excel at the perfect living of Life as designed by the divine
148. God is good
149. Good dominates my every experience.
150. I am a strong being with many abilities and skills.
151. In every moment, I am inspired to take the right action, morally, ethically and spiritually.
152. I am focused on finding the best parts of nature and enjoying them.
153. God knows my needs and meets them.
154. Divinity dwells in me as the living, breathing spirit of me. Therefore, I am now whole, perfect and complete in every way.
155. I know the people around me are also magical forces of nature.
156. God lives inside my heart and in my subconscious
157. My life is part of an everlasting fabric that connects the world together.
158. I am part of a beautiful world that welcomes me.
159. God within me is mighty, powerful and unstoppable.
160. I believe in the creative power of nature to transform my life.
161. I am Divinely led, guided and inspired in all I think, do and say.
162. My life is enriched by the experiences of other people
163. Study, prayer, and meditation prepare me to live my faith.
164. I am a force of nature with the ability to control my circumstances.
165. My faith motivates me to take care of my well-being.

166. My faith defines my life and gives me purpose. I call upon my faith for routine chores and small gestures, as well as great demands.
167. My faith encourages me to give more. I share my time and resources with my family, friends, and community.
168. I am sheltered and enveloped by the perfect Peace of God.
169. I build a strong foundation that inspires and empowers me.
170. My faith fills me with gratitude. I give thanks for my blessings.
171. With you oh mighty and divine one, I feel at peace, ease and joyful
172. Nature gives me strength and energy, so I can enjoy the world around me.
173. My faith increases my patience. I accept delays and setbacks as a natural part of life. I remain calm and adapt to whatever circumstances come my way.
174. My faith plays a guiding role in my daily life. I put my beliefs into action.
175. My faith shapes the way I speak. I choose gracious words that convey my respect and affection for others. I promote peace and harmony through tolerance
176. I am sheltered by the mercy of Spirit
177. I develop the courage and wisdom to overcome challenges, and use my spiritual gifts to serve others and create a better life for myself.
178. Understanding and appreciating nature makes me happy.
179. I build a strong spiritual foundation that inspires and empowers me.
180. Today I am centered in my heart, and closer to Spirit.
181. I am perfectly blessed and I am a perfect blessing for the world.
182. Today, I recognize that I am a powerful force of nature. My life is filled with amazing opportunities made possible by nature.

183. I know that I am an everlasting force and part of a miraculous world.
184. Everywhere I go, everything I see, everything I experience provides visible proof that I am supported and sustained by the entirety of creation.
185. My heart and life are open to receive every divine blessing
186. The Spirit of God within knows the perfect way to answer and respond to my every need and desire. Therefore, all my needs are met.
187. Now is the time for my good
188. I patiently and respectfully ask for Divine guidance on anything and everything.
189. I am anchored in love. I am buoyed by love. The wings of love lift me into perfect communion with all life everywhere.
190. I live in the moment and am grateful for all my life experiences. All of them.
191. I see myself and the spark of divinity in others.
192. Today, I demonstrate my faith. My actions reflect my beliefs.

CHAPTER NINE

POSITIVE AFFIRMATIONS FOR THE CAREER MINDED

1. I further my career with every action I take.
2. I have my dream job.
3. I love every day that I work.
4. My career brings me closer to my family.
5. My job brings me financial abundance.
6. My coworkers love being around me.
7. My boss values the work I do.
8. I am a valued employee.
9. My clients appreciate and value my work.
10. I attract new clients every day.
11. My positive attitude, confidence and hard work naturally draws in new opportunities.
12. I am enthusiastic and excited about my work.
13. My enthusasm about my job is contagious.
14. My workplace is peaceful and full of love.
15. I make decisions easily.
16. I speak positively about my coworkers and they respond by speaking positively about me
17. Work and Career Affirmations
18. My job adds satisfaction and fulfillment to my life.
19. I am exactly where I want to be. My career provides me the right opportunities to grow.
20. I am valued and appreciated at my workplace. My voice is always heard.
21. I ask for meaningful work and perform it with the greatest diligence and attention.

22. My work has a profound impact on this world.
23. Right now, the job I am looking for is looking for me.
24. I am a great employee. Any employer is lucky to have me.
25. I am an asset to any organization, and I prove it in every interview.
26. Every time I interview for a job, I exude confidence and energy.
27. Amazing opportunities are appearing in my life out of nowhere.
28. I am ready for my interviews. I am confident in my interviews. I am successful in my interviews.
29. I am creating the career of my dreams.
30. Career change is an opportunity to have the career I want. This time I choose a great career for me.
31. No more excuses! I deserve a job that fulfills me, and I am ready to find it.
32. I committed to my happiness in this job search, and my determination pays off.
33. Every time I say 'no' to the wrong job, I get closer to the perfect job.
34. I see myself in my ideal job.
35. I act with confidence and have a plan, and I accept that plans are open to change.
36. I love challenges because they bring out the best in me.
37. I easily and effortlessly learn new system and processes.
38. I am kind, loving, and compassionate. I truly care for other people.
39. It comes naturally to be confident in myself. I don't need to question my confidence.
40. I don't need to be perfect. I am already good enough and I am worthy of a great life already.
41. I do not have a need to compare myself to other people. I only judge myself by my own standards of success. I am enough just the way I am.

42. I channel love, positivity, and energy to all the people around me.
43. Positive Affirmations for Women While at Work
44. I practice self-care and recognize when I need to take a break. I feel good about taking care of myself.
45. I am successful and confident in my abilities to do my job.
46. I am a competent member of the team. I have the knowledge and skills that I need right now.
47. I move at the perfect pace. I do not need to speed up or slow down.
48. I embrace success. The words "I can't" are not something I say. I refuse to believe even my own excuses. I am unstoppable.
49. I take my goals seriously. I am aware that my time on earth is finite. I respect my life by doing the things I love.
50. I refuse to overcommit myself. I am able to say "no" when I need to. I protect my time because I deserve it and it is invaluable.
51. My work is a self-transformative process that brings me inner peace, proper health, and prosperity.
52. I'm almost at the finish line. I know I have what it takes to meet my goals.
53. My hard work, humility, and persistence will pay off. None of my work is going to waste.
54. The passion I have for my work allows me to create true value. I am lucky to have a job that provides me with the finances I need to live a good life.
55. I work extremely hard and always do my personal best. I believe in myself and I know I can do anything. I deserve all of the positive things that come my way in life.
56. The work that I do benefits the society in which I live, and I am a valuable part of my community.
57. I do not give up when things get difficult. I keep working until I finish what I started.

58. My work is fulfilling, inspiring, and enriching. I am not only helping myself, but I am also helping others.
59. I see myself reaching the pinnacle of success as I envision it and work hard every day until I am where I want to be in my career
60. I bring something unique to the table that no one else can and that makes me uniquely valuable to my company.
61. I am a capable leader. Others are attracted to my charisma at work and look up to me during times of crisis.
62. I stay true to my values and my authentic self. I do not compromise for anyone else. My success will come without compromise.
63. I do not need to prove my worth. My work is enough for people to see its value. People recognize my worth without having to be told.
64. Other people's successes empower me to keep growing. I am happy for anyone who accomplishes their goals and I will strive to continue to accomplish mine.
65. I cultivate a sense of gratitude and thank others for their kindness at work.
66. I appreciate my education, and the opportunity to do meaningful work.
67. No matter how busy I am, I am still actively involved in my community. I comfort a friend who is feeling blue and help an elderly neighbor with yard work.
68. My most important mission in life is to stay true to myself.
69. I embrace the energy I receive from work and my coworkers.
70. Even when unpopular, I choose to protect and uphold my beliefs because they keep me honest.
71. Sometimes my coworkers cause new employees to feel out of place. I avoid joining them by helping new persons to feel welcome.
72. Self-discipline is my forte. I conduct myself at work in a professional manner

73. I know how to strike a healthy balance in life. At the workplace, work is my priority and at home, family is my priority.
74. I am known for being industrious and seizing whatever opportunities that are available.
75. I am a master salesman for the company I work for
76. Career to me is a means to an end. That end is happiness and fulfillment of potential and my career is providing it to me in abundance.
77. I am always ready to learn and grow in my job!
78. Diligence in work, honesty in attitude and a positive frame of mind open up new horizons for me in my career.
79. The fruits of my labor are always so sweet and rewarding
80. My main aim is satisfaction of my customers and I strive my best to achieve that aim.
81. I accept constructive feedback and put it work for my benefit
82. Today I see the ways this job contributes to my growth.
83. I work hard at what I do. I work smart in wisdom and application of skills and I deserve the accolades I earn
84. I am passionate about my job. I recognize and seize opportunities as and when they appear.
85. The customers I cater to on behalf of the company love and trust me and as a result, my order book is overflowing with orders.
86. I am always enthusiastic and my enthusiasm rubs off on my co-workers and this results in a productive work day for all of us.
87. I always attract the best projects and the best people to execute them because of my positive mental attitude.
88. I am not frustrated as I have the freedom to either keep this job or find a better job whenever I want to.
89. My career is what I make of it and today, I have made the choice to make it a happy and successful experience.

90. Today I see the ways this job contributes to my financial well-being.
91. My career is mine alone and today, I am taking ownership of it
92. I know that I am blessed with the job that I have. I remind myself to be content with what I have.
93. Today, I choose to focus on positivity and enjoy the beauty that surrounds me. I take a walk around my neighborhood to marvel at nature and renew my energy.
94. I became a (insert current job role) to make a difference and today I am seizing every chance to do so
95. As I align my career with my true talents, passions and skills, the money I desire and the happiness from fulfillment flows to me
96. I am happy that the work I do benefits me as well as the society I live in.
97. I am a valued person at my workplace and my voice is always heard respectfully.
98. I climb the corporate ladder with integrity and confidence
99. I acknowledge my potential in this place and celebrate my accomplishments.
100. I am able to balance my career with my family life so that both are in harmony with each other.
101. I mold my current career to match my life goals
102. I am attracting into my life my dream job and most suitable work for me.
103. I am manifesting my dream job.
104. I always see possibilities, I refuse to see dead ends in my career.
105. I am enjoying working in my dream job.
106. Outside of work, I have a strong support system. I value my family and friends. I let them know that they are a vital part of my life.

107. I am aware that the Universe is making all the perfect arrangement for my dream job.
108. I am not overtly focused on just myself and my career growth. I share my riches, time and ideas with others.
109. A great company has offered me a dream job
110. I have a great relationship with the people I work with as well as my boss.
111. I have found a lucrative job and I love working there
112. Today, my affirmations are attracting to me the job I enjoy doing
113. Thinking about my recent victories builds my confidence and inspires me to aim higher.
114. Today, I declare that I am working in a successful company, at an excellent workplace with wonderful people
115. I am attracting the right job into my life
116. Today I choose to grow and get better through collaboration with my colleagues.
117. I am manifesting a great job, which I love and enjoy, and my job is bringing me a lot of money.
118. Doors of opportunities are open to me this day
119. I am the engine of my career success
120. I am making the right connections at work
121. I am a world-class (insert dream job position) and I am presented with the opportunity to prove it every day
122. I have found the dream work for me. I am at the right place, and I like the people that I work with.
123. Right now, I am working at my dream job.&
124. I manage work stress by listening to music that eases my tension and cheers me up.
125. Today and every day, I use my talents in productive ways
126. My work ethic ensures that I get regular promotions and monetary incentives.
127. I take full responsibility for my work.

128. I am excited to have this job and I work diligently to make the most of it.
129. There are no limits to the greatness I accomplish
130. My empathy for others is alive even at work. I pitch in when a coworker is swamped and take time to listen when a friend is going through a difficult time.
131. I always work for amazing bosses.
132. I take good care of my juniors and guide them appropriately. I am friendly with my colleagues and respectful to my seniors.
133. I am working at my dream job
134. I open myself to receive the offer to work in dream job
135. I put a lot of worth and value on committing to the things I believe in.
136. My job does not define me, but I have the power define my job
137. Today I see the ways this job contributes to my happiness.
138. My ideal employment is coming to me right now.
139. I love and enjoy my work because I find fulfilment in it
140. My knowledge, wisdom, and skills help me to make valuable contribution to my job, society and provide for my family.
141. I am the director of my career and I take the initiative to have the career I want
142. I am working in a job which I love and I am receiving very handsome salary
143. The ambience of my workplace is non-toxic and as a result, I grow in my career
144. I have unlimited potential and my dream job is looking for me
145. I am working at a job I love and enjoy, and which is very satisfying and fulfilling in every day
146. I love and enjoy my job. My job is is bringing me a lot of money and feeding my passion

147. When career challenges arise, I keep my attention focused on the good things going on in my workplace.
148. I am confident of my skills and abilities to attract my dream job
149. I am a great employee. Any employer is lucky to have me.
150. I am an asset to any organization, and I prove it in every interview.
151. I am appreciated and rewarded well wherever I work.
152. I am fully myself and completely authentic in my career.
153. It's not what I do, but how I do it... I treat every task as an opportunity to create more beauty, abundance and joy.
154. Today, I abandon my old work habits and take up new, more positive ones
155. I am doing my best in my career and giving my everything without reservation.
156. Amazing career opportunities are appearing in my life out of nowhere.
157. The Universe is making perfect arrangements to find right employment for me
158. I am attracting most suitable job opportunities
159. My career happiness is a choice I make everyday.
160. I am open to new opportunities that lead me to get my dream job.
161. I am confident radiating who I am in all situations at work
162. I love my career as it allows me to grow as well as makes me financially abundant.
163. My mistakes do not define me or dictate my future success.
164. I deserve to have an exciting, rewarding career. It is so much fulfilling
165. I am deeply fulfilled by all that I do.
166. What I do in my job makes a difference to at least one person in the world. I work in the knowledge of this truth
167. I unselfishly share my gifts with the world and give others permission to do the same.

168. I teach my peers to believe in me by believing in myself
169. The joy I find in my career is reflected in my overall happiness.
170. I am grateful for the discomfort of growing in my career, as I expand myself to create all that I've wished for
171. I am energetic and enthusiastic about my job. Confidence is my second nature
172. I have the courage to go after what I truly want
173. Right now, the job I am looking for is looking for me.
174. Everyday, I tap into more of my potential
175. I choose community over competition in my work and my life.
176. I serve others willingly, gladly and gratefully.
177. Harmony permeates my experience, and my work flows in productive and joyful ways.
178. I deserve to work in a dream job.
179. In my career and in my life, change is constant. I accept change and make the most of it.
180. I have everything I need to create my own opportunities at work
181. I manifest unexpected opportunities every day because I am aligned with my calling.
182. I am calm and comfortable speaking out in front of my colleagues. I have confidence in myself, thus, I relate easily with them.
183. I have found my ideal employment
184. I am opening my consciousness to a greater prosperity and part of that prosperity is an increased salary.
185. I am always open to opportunities to get me an ideal employment
186. Today, I am attracting into my life the best and most suitable job for me
187. I am creating and building the career of my dreams.

188. I am ready for my interviews. I am confident in my interviews. I am successful in my interviews.
189. I accept constructive criticism and welcome self-improvement
190. I am at a workplace that I love, and my job gives me satisfaction and good salary
191. I am now manifesting an opportunity for a wonderful and well-paying job
192. I offer constructive criticism to help others around me.

CHAPTER TEN

POSITIVE AFFIRMATIONS FOR CREATIVITY

1. I tap into the universal source of inspiration to boost my creativity .
2. I access and I use the vibrant energy that surrounds me on all levels.
3. I channel the positive life forces around me to increase my own creativity and become amore expressive individual.
4. I summon the creative energy of the stars and planets to surround and fill me.
5. Every being has creative energy from the universe and I have access to the source
6. I embrace new sources of energy as I grow and become stronger. The earth, water, and air are filled with powerful forces I can use.
7. Being positive improves my creativity.
8. I draw inspiration from the world around me It provides me with strength, so my abilities grow and change.
9. I am a powerful creator, and I create the life that I want starting today.
10. The artist is already present within me.
11. I am inspired, creative and productive.
12. I come up with new and innovative ideas easily.
13. I am a visionary.
14. Great ideas come to me easily.
15. I am part of an infinite universe with an endless supply of creativity.

16. Doing repetitive tasks frees my mind to consider creative solutions to problems.
17. I am a magnet for innovative ideas.
18. An endless reservoir of creativity lies within me.
19. The beautiful universe around me has abundant energy for me to use.
20. I find original solutions to problems.
21. I have an adventurous, imaginative mind.
22. I am grateful for the creative ideas that come to me.
23. I follow my creative inclinations.
24. I love inventing exciting new ways of doing things.
25. I am awake and see the world through fresh eyes.
26. I have infinite creative potential.
27. Today, I recognize the energy around me and appreciate the creative it provides me.
28. I will come up with amazing new ideas
29. Being creative makes me feel so alive.
30. Creative inspiration follows me wherever I go.
31. Ideas are starting to flow freely from my mind
32. I am creative and have the willpower to make use of my talents.
33. I always have lots of unique ideas for solving problems.
34. I am finding it easier and easier to come up with new ideas
35. I am surrounded by revitalizing forces that spread over me and reach every part of me.
36. I increase my inventiveness in all that I do.
37. My creativity is increasing
38. Today I am making time to create.
39. I am always tapped into my creative energy
40. My creative juices are a natural stimulant.
41. I am a brilliant and successful artist.
42. Today, I am happy that I have values to help me make wise decisions when innovating.
43. My imagination is becoming stronger and stronger

44. I am a creative thinker.
45. I know that being creatively true to myself always pays off in the end.
46. I am comfortable with alone thinking.
47. Divine inspiration surrounds me.
48. Creativity flows through every cell in my body.
49. I can feel new sources of creative energy enter my body and mind.
50. My creativity fills me with passion and purpose.
51. I have a fertile imagination.
52. Every creative thought I express provides me with great joy.
53. I am a fount of ingenuity.
54. I will tap into my creative energy
55. I attract brilliant ideas
56. I exercise my imagination at every opportunity.
57. Creative ideas come to me regularly.
58. I take inspired action to keep my creative spark alive.
59. Everything I create is inventive and unique.
60. I am clever and creative in all that I do.
61. Creativity makes it easy for me to step into my uncomfortable zone
62. I am easily able to come up with fresh, new ideas.
63. Creative energy flows through me at all times.
64. I choose to create.
65. My creative spirit has no boundaries
66. I easily tap into the Creative Force whenever I need to.
67. The abundant universe the resource to keep my creative spark alive.
68. I am an unlimited creative being.
69. My creative source never runs dry.
70. Brilliant ideas come to me all the time.
71. Creatively, I am spontaneous; I surprise even myself.
72. My creative energy radiates outwardly to myself and the people I meet.

73. I am creatively expressing my highest potential.
74. The art of mindfulness ignites my creative spark.
75. Every day I become more creative and inventive.
76. I am in love with my unique creative expression.
77. I am immensely grateful for my creative abilities.
78. I am inspired by the beauty in my life and all around me.
79. I am a creative problem solver.
80. My environment supports my creative thinking
81. I am grateful for the energy that feeds my imagination.
82. I am efficient and imaginative in my work.
83. I am open to new experiences
84. I give myself room for self- expression.
85. Being creative is one of the top priorities in my life, and I practice this feeling every day.
86. Every moment of every day I am becoming more and more inventive.
87. My creative thoughts boost my confidence and courage in my abilities
88. I am a creative problem solver.
89. I am endowed with great creativity and intelligence.
90. I easily connect with the infinite creativity of the universe.
91. Innovative thoughts keep me on my toes
92. Being creative is one of my great joys in life.
93. I give thanks for the creative inspiration I receive daily.
94. I am a naturally artistic individual
95. My creative energy is limitless.
96. I employ my power in inventive and helpful ways.
97. I am incredibly creative and inspired.
98. Divine inspiration blesses every day of my life.
99. I always follow where inspiration leads.
100. I exercise innovative thinking at all times.
101. Fresh ideas come quickly and easily to me.
102. Every day I let my imagination soar to new heights.
103. I am a powerful and resourceful creator.

104. I find inventive solutions for each problem I am present with.
105. I open myself to a life of creativity.
106. My mind is flexible
107. I am an innovative thinker.
108. My imagination and creativity are my dynamic duo
109. I create new masterpieces every day.
110. The wellspring of creativity runs deep in me
111. I express my creativity whenever possible.
112. I have abundant creative talent.
113. I am always developing great new ways of doing things.
114. I am a creator and an innovator
115. I easily tap the imaginative resources of my mind.
116. I love exercising my artistic side.
117. I expand my understanding of things and this feeds my imagination.
118. I'm ready to share my authentic expression.
119. My creativity is growing
120. I am imaginative and creative in all that I do.
121. I have a wealth of good ideas.
122. I easily find novel solutions to problems.
123. The natural beauty of life insures my creativity
124. I am ever receptive to the inspiration the universe sends me.
125. I am an innovator. My ideas are inspiring.
126. I am full of infinite, creative energy.
127. I wake up with good ideas every single day
128. I am continually developing new, innovative ideas.
129. I enjoy my natural creativity.
130. My creativity flows freely.
131. I allow my creative genius to shine.
132. Great new ideas come to me every day.
133. I love inventing things.
134. I will tap into my imagination

135. I approach all problems in an inspired and resourceful way.
136. I am becoming highly creative
137. I feel creative and inspired at work.
138. My creative self wants to come out and play.
139. Creative ideas just flow out of my mind naturally
140. I have a great imagination.
141. I have a powerful imagination
142. I employ lateral thinking in all that I do.
143. I will unleash my creativity today
144. I am confident and skilled in my creative work.
145. Creativity comes naturally to me
146. I allow my creative energy to flow freely at all times.
147. I have endless creativity
148. I am very resourceful and inventive.
149. I am effortlessly creative at all times
150. I can get into a creative state of mind whenever I want.
151. I love and embrace my inner creative child.
152. Today, I am filled with infinite, creative energy.
153. I play and create with the joyful exuberance of a child.
154. I am always thinking of new, original ways to do things.
155. My imagination runs wild
156. I find creative solutions to problems every day.
157. I am a wellspring of creativity.
158. My creative mind is my best resource for overcoming challenges
159. I exercise my creative genius every day.
160. I am infinitely creative.
161. I have a fantastic imagination
162. I love expressing myself creatively.
163. I am always developing as an artist.
164. I am open to perfecting my creativity potential
165. I have an endless supply of creativity.
166. I am one with the creative flow of life.
167. My creativity overpowers my fears.

168. I have instant access to unlimited ingenuity.
169. The universe is my creative playground
170. I am incredibly creative and imaginative.
171. I love losing myself in the zone of creative thought.
172. I find original solutions for all difficulties in my life.
173. Nurturing my creative mind is a priority.
174. I am a creative genius.
175. My creativity is for the betterment of mankind.
176. I honor my creative genius.
177. I am inventive and resourceful.
178. I love inventing original new products.
179. I love exercising original thinking.
180. I can always count on my imagination for inspiring ideas.
181. New ideas are always coming to me
182. I love having an outlet for my artistic abilities.
183. I am forever grateful for my imaginative mind.
184. My creative mind frees me from habitual thinking.
185. My mind is wired for creativity
186. I increase my creativity by being clearly focused in the present.
187. Living a creative life is important to me; it makes me a healthier, happier person.
188. I invent new things that are inspiring
189. I express my unique creativity in all that I do.
190. Fresh new ideas come to me daily.

CHAPTER ELEVEN

POSITIVE AFFIRMATIONS FOR WOMEN

1. I am happy, healthy, and centered.
2. Change provides me opportunity.
3. My life is an adventure.
4. Good enough is good enough.
5. Feelings are not facts.
6. I have abundant energy.
7. My child is happy and healthy.
8. Let go of "what if
9. I will not live in reaction to my child.
10. Balance in life is what I strive for.
11. I will take time to put myself first.
12. I will act after thought, not on instinct.
13. Calm is my primary state of being.
14. I am content.
15. Principles guide me. Not a moments fancy.
16. I give myself permission to take personal time.
17. Would I expect this of anyone else?
18. I am unique and a gift to the world.
19. I am at peace with my body and accept it as it is. It was created to do amazing things.
20. I love living in my unique female body. It has features that are distinctive and make me who I am.
21. I am attractive just as I am. I don't need to change anything. I'm not perfect, but I am still beautiful.
22. I love my body and I take care of it through healthy eating and exercise. I respect my body and am thankful for all it can do.

23. I am responsible for what happens to my body, so I treat it with love, respect, and care.
24. I exercise my body daily with ease and am amazed at the ways it can bend, move, stretch, and pose.
25. I am a strong, confident woman and will only continue to become stronger.
26. I am patient with my body when it needs rest, healing, and recovery.
27. I respect my body's needs and treat it with the kindness that it deserves.
28. I choose to release love, happiness and gratitude into the world today. Life is precious and beautiful, and I choose to focus on the positive.
29. I am grateful for this wonderful day and the endless possibilities it has to offer. I know something great is in store for me.
30. No matter what goes on today, I know the truth that I am a radiant, powerful, and free woman.
31. I embrace my best self today. I live in a way that brings tranquility, joy, and pleasure to myself and others.
32. I know I am alive for a reason. Today, I honor my purpose and inspire people around me to do the same.
33. I don't need anyone else or anything to complete me because I am already complete just as I am.
34. I am beautiful and I am worthy of every beautiful thing in this world.
35. I am overflowing with renewed confidence every day. I continue to grow and become a stronger woman for myself and for the people around me.
36. I accept that I cannot change the past. I focus on my future and move forward in my life. My past does not define who I am today.

37. I do one thing every day to make consistent progress toward my dreams. I surpass other people's expectations because I am exceptional.
38. I choose to learn from the positive and negative events of the past so that I continue to make progress towards my bright future.
39. I do not need to control everything around me. I focus on allowing the best things to happen. I know that whatever is supposed to be will be.
40. I am cultured and smart, yet able to stay humble.
41. Because of my high self-esteem, I easily accept compliments and give them in return.
42. I deserve everything that is good. I do not have any need for misery and suffering.
43. I accept my past mistakes and let them go. They don't define me. I move forward with confidence in my essential goodness and good judgment.
44. My mind is full of caring, healthy, positive, and loving thoughts which transform into my life experiences.
45. My voice matters and I am confident to speak up when I want to. People listen to me because my words are valuable.
46. Success is possible for me because I have the right opportunities, and I take advantage of them when I see them. I know the path I need to take in order to succeed.
47. I have more than enough value to offer in my job. I continue to flourish and gain experience and succeed to levels that I never expected.
48. My mind is focused, and I have clarity in all that I do at work. I do not succumb to distractions.
49. Others recognize my work for its excellence, and I am proud to call it my own.
50. I am on my way to greatness. I go the extra mile to meet people whom I admire and respect. I take one step farther than anyone else around me.

51. I avoid fretting about past disappointments or comparing myself to others.
52. I realize that I have all that I need to be happy in this present moment.
53. I wake up every day with a restored sense of well-being.
54. I am focused. I give my full attention to each task, whether I am setting the dinner table or writing a computer program.
55. I embrace the new day with love in my heart.
56. I take care of my body and mind so that I am strong enough to give to others..
57. I have new energy and a deeper understanding of my surroundings.
58. I am awakened with appreciation and stirred up in awe of the wonders of my body
59. I love the beautiful world and appreciate all my blessings as well as my place in it
60. I organize my schedule while remaining flexible enough to take advantage of promising opportunities that come my way
61. My sense of wonder at my strengths and discovery of my potentials are restored, so I can explore new experiences.
62. I am secure in my perception of my place in the world.
63. I volunteer in my community and extend my hospitality to newcomers and old friends.
64. My nurturing love grows with each moment I spend on this planet.
65. I set specific goals that guide my actions and add value to my life.
66. Today, I remember my love of the world is renewed every day.
67. I find new meaning and joy in daily tasks.
68. I value my family and friends. I let them know that they are a vital part of my life.
69. My love is daily extended to my family, friends, coworkers and others.

70. I appreciate the people, places, experiences and events that shape my life.
71. I appreciate each person and the lessons our interactions bring
72. I am grateful for the chance to change and find recovery every day.
73. I embrace the energy I receive from friends and family. Together, we form a strong and powerful group that has unique capabilities and talents.
74. I am stronger and better because I attract positive powers into my life.
75. I remind my family that it is my responsibility to be forthright even with my them.
76. I know how to value my present, accept my past, and plan for my future with love in my heart.
77. I avoid viewing the decisions of people I care about as acceptable when they are misaligned with my beliefs.
78. Each day I encounter family, friends, and acquaintances. I am conscious of differences in thoughts and actions and respect them. But I avoid adopting them just for validation.
79. When family members make questionable decisions, I hold them accountable
80. I am mature enough to know that genuine friendships are able to withstand tension that comes from differences in opinion.
81. My body and mind are connected to the deepest parts of the universe. They are renewed each night as I dream.
82. I have something special to offer my family and the world.
83. I let my friends know the lines I am unwilling to cross. I am happy that they respect my point of view.
84. I am a very brave, strong woman
85. I deserve to be happy and loved
86. I spread joy with every step I take on my journey
87. My true friends appreciate me even when our thoughts differ. Our diversity helps to keep our relationship interesting.
88. I am the better half. I am better in everything I do.

89. I take care of my body in healthy ways.
90. I embrace my wrinkles and lines of wisdom.
91. I recognize that opportunities exist to celebrate life anew each and every day.
92. I reconnect with my dreams and these dreams help me renew my love of the physical world.
93. The fountain of youth lies in my heart, mind and soul.
94. It's okay to live my dream today and to be a little selfish
95. I am thankful for every part of my body.
96. I am in a constant state of progress.
97. I love myself, respect myself and accept myself exactly as I am.
98. I am attractive as I am.
99. I adopt a healthy outlook on matters that relate to getting older.
100. I am doing my best every single day and it is enough.
101. I embrace the female cycles that my body experiences.
102. I get older gracefully.
103. I am wiser and wiser each day.
104. I am worthy of love and respect
105. I am the perfect age today.
106. I take full responsibility for my wellness.
107. I wear confidence in my smile and in the way I move my body.
108. I have a healthy relationship with time in terms of my age
109. My love for the world is nurtured by the universe. I am part of a magical collection of beings who are changing and growing each day.
110. I may be older but I feel young and alive
111. I give myself permission to be relaxed and happy
112. I am not afraid of getting older. Instead, I step into the next stage of my life with ease and confidence.
113. I choose today to begin to materialize my dream
114. My life becomes richer in meaning through the years.

115. I nourish my body with healthy thoughts each day.
116. I recognize the wisdom, strength, and compassion that within me.
117. I am thankful to be alive, to be well and to be breathing
118. I am honored to have so many friends in my life
119. I am well supported by the female tribe.
120. I let my love for myself increase each day
121. No success is too small to celebrate, and I revel in the tiny wins today.
122. I connect with my inner goddess who loves to shine.
123. I am always safe and protected
124. I benefit from the wisdom of the women who have come before me
125. It isn't selfish to be kind to myself.
126. I have a sisterhood of women who nurture and support me
127. I am at peace in my own body
128. I celebrate who I am and who I am becoming with each passing day.
129. I am a woman of substance. I take interest in everything. I take great care to develop my personality.
130. I deserve a loving, supportive partner
131. I am a sympathetic yet assertive and demanding boss and treat my employees equitably. I get the best out of each employee
132. I celebrate every aspect of my life with utmost joy.
133. I love myself and treat myself with kindness.
134. I allow my inner goddess to rock her magic.
135. Today I start loving myself more
136. I am amazed by the perfect creation of my physical being.
137. I am a loving and nurturing sister. I care for and dote on my brother.
138. I enjoy being a woman
139. I discover true joy with being a woman, even as I get older.
140. I align with the dreams of my inner goddess.

141. All my dreams are destined to come true
142. I am open to new adventures in life.
143. I commit to my success and I do not allow myself to be intimidated
144. I have been blessed with qualities that uplift others and even on my hardest days, I am the perfect mother for my children.
145. I am unique and complete by just being me
146. I am a productive employee. I take my job seriously and always give my best.
147. I am blessed to be a woman. I draw on my feminine qualities and gifts for success.
148. I can handle anything that comes into my life
149. As a woman, I deserve success as much as any man who works hard out there.
150. My body shape is perfect in the way that it's intended to be
151. I am so in love right now with my true self
152. I listen to my body's needs attentively.
153. I embrace every imperfection that I perceive in my appearance
154. I am confident in my sexuality.
155. I am blessed with the gift of living and I appreciate this
156. I find deep inner peace within myself as I am
157. I embrace my curves. I love being me.
158. I am driven and motivated for success and in shows in my work ethics
159. I enjoy expressing myself as a woman totally.
160. I am a strong, confident and capable woman.
161. I am gentle with myself
162. I wear my confidence as a woman with pride.
163. Every cell in my body is perfect, complete and whole
164. I love myself fully, including the way I look
165. I embrace my life each and every day, even as I get older.

166. I am committed to my success and will not back down. I enjoy taking action when I have a goal so I can acquire the lifestyle that I dream of.
167. I am well supported by my loved ones and the people in my community.
168. My breast size is perfect in the way that it's intended to be.
169. My self-esteem is high because I honor who I am
170. I embrace my grey hair with grace
171. I am enough as I am
172. I strive to improve myself
173. My inner goddess is magic, crystals and sunshine
174. I am the best friend that anyone can have. For me, friendship is the ultimate relationship.
175. I discover everlasting beauty from the inside-out.
176. I choose to understand and forgive myself
177. I enjoy being in this female body.
178. I am a being of unconditional love and compassion
179. I am a loving and caring wife. My partner is my soul mate. We complement each other.
180. I have persistence in what I believe
181. I can do anything that I put my mind to
182. I am a model daughter. I love and respect my parents and discharge faithfully my duties toward them.
183. I appreciate every moment of my life
184. I am perfect as I am.
185. I love and enjoy being the best of myself
186. I am a woman of love. My touch heals all wounds.
187. I combine feminity and intelligence beautifully
188. I adore motherhood. I am an ideal mother and my children love me.
189. It's okay to be a powerful woman
190. With every breath I become more peaceful

191. I am calm when I am faced with conflict. I can brush off negativity easily, and I can agree to disagree. I enjoy being the bigger person and taking the high road.

CHAPTER TWELVE

POSITIVE AFFIRMATIONS FOR MEN

1. I am respected and appreciated and deservedly so.
2. I am moving closer to my dreams.
3. I surrender my ego and pride to the universe. I embrace humility
4. I am outgoing and charismatic.
5. I have a positive body image.
6. Today, I deserve to have a great job success.
7. I know that I am worthy of financial stability.
8. I am grateful for the abundance I have.
9. I am connected to my inner emotions and I am not ashamed of this
10. My confidence grows stronger each day.
11. I love myself and I accept myself as I am.
12. I love being a father. I am an ideal father and my children love me.
13. I am brave and I courageously take on my responsibilities
14. I can change any negative perceptions I have about myself
15. I am a good person.
16. I am a great provider for my family.
17. I am the creator of my life. I refuse to be stereotyped into a role
18. I am worthy of happiness, wealth and peace. I can't control others.
19. I am successful, prosperous, healthy, and happy.
20. I am a man of substance. I am interested in everything.
21. I feel sexy, charming and attractive.
22. I am assertive and at the same time, considerate about others.

23. I am a strong advocate for myself. I strongly believe in my abilities.
24. I am not a failure. I learn from any challenges I encounter.
25. In my field of work, I am a productive employee. I take my job seriously and always give my best.
26. I bravely strive to better myself in every way
27. I am proud and happy to be the man that I am
28. I am strong, courageous and independent. I live my truth
29. I am in control of my life.
30. I attract new business opportunities easily.
31. As a child, I love and respect my parents and faithfully discharge my duties toward them.
32. I treat myself right because I love myself.
33. I am confident in my looks. I am a sexy and attractive man.
34. People genuinely enjoy being around me because of my positive energy
35. Every day I am getting more confident I myself. I take on new adventures
36. I am looking healthier and stronger every day because ai am making the right eating choices
37. I balance my masculine and feminine energies.
38. I will continue to grow and learn.
39. I am everything a son can be. I make my parents proud in everything I do.
40. Whatever I am called to do, leadership comes to me instinctively
41. I am bold and confident. I refuse to be pressured into making poor choices
42. Today, I am grateful for the man I am becoming.
43. I am living the life I always wanted.
44. I am a successful and thriving family man. I am a loving husband and a doting father.
45. In my relationship, I am the other half. I am best in everything I do.

46. I am manly in my appearance, caring in my attitude and loving in my personality.
47. I am in touch with my emotions and I am not ashamed to be vulnerable
48. I am connected to my inner motivation. I wake up each morning with intention and purpose.
49. Today is meaningful, important, and special. I live it with purpose
50. I radiate love with smiles and I feel it reflected back to me
51. I love myself in a healthy and wholesome way
52. Health is a priority for me. I take good care of my body.
53. Today, I base my happiness on my own accomplishments and the blessings I've been given.
54. I am a loving person. I give out love and I receive love unconditionally.
55. My emotions and feelings are worthy of attention
56. I am excited for what is to come. Because the gest days are ahead
57. I love, appreciate and value the person I am becoming
58. I am smart, generous and good at my job.
59. Creative energy surges through me and leads me to new and brilliant ideas.
60. I am worthy of love and deserve the good kind of love
61. I love the way I look and I put in the work to look good
62. Success and wealth come effortlessly to me.
63. I have great ideas that are transformative
64. I am not aggressive. I am assertive and strong.
65. I listen to my needs and prioritize self-care because I deserve it
66. Happiness is a choice. I am choosing to be happy today.
67. Today, I am closer to making my dreams come true than I was yesterday.
68. I am a man who creates responses to circumstances not just reactions.

69. Everything that is happening now is happening for my ultimate good.
70. I am a man who receives wisdom from my subconscious 24/7.
71. I am blessed with an incredible family and wonderful friends.
72. I actively listen to what other men say without interrupting them.
73. I have all the qualities of a strong man.
74. I am guided in my every step by the spirit who leads me towards what I must know and do.
75. Today, I abandon my old habits and take up new, more positive ones.
76. I have been given endless talents which I begin to utilize today.
77. As a leader, I am a sympathetic yet assertive and demanding boss and treat my employees equitably.
78. I am a man of substance.
79. I am a glorious creature. I radiate beauty, charm, and grace.
80. My efforts are being supported by the universe; my dreams manifest into reality before my eyes.
81. I am the ideal male figure.
82. I am actively involved in building my community
83. I can do anything I put my mind to.
84. I love and nurture the people in my life with strength and empathy.
85. Today and every day going forward, I acknowledge my own self-worth; my confidence is soaring.
86. My thoughts are filled with positivity and my life is plentiful with prosperity.
87. I radiate with self-confidence and a charming energy.
88. I am a man of my word.
89. As a provider, I seek to provide for my loved ones.
90. My fears of tomorrow are simply melting away.
91. I am resilient, nothing really breaks me

92. I am the creator of my entire life and experiences
93. Successful people are attracted to me.
94. I forgive those who have harmed me in my past and peacefully detach from them.
95. My marriage/relationship is becoming stronger, deeper, and more stable each day.
96. I believe in myself.
97. I am open to abundance, joy, pleasure and positive experiences in life.
98. I am ready to create amazing memories that will be worth remembering
99. My future is an ideal projection of what I envision now.
100. I am the best male friend that anyone can have. For me, friendship is the ultimate relationship.
101. I am naturally masculine, graceful and handsome.
102. I am a giving man who knows how to make others feel happy about life.
103. I am highly resilient. I can withstand tough times
104. I am the architect of my life; I build its foundation and choose its contents.
105. I define my own happiness and success; not the world or society dictates to me
106. I am a confident man with a hunger and desire to achieve my goals every day.
107. All the things that are happening in my life are to benefit me.
108. I am superior to negative thoughts and low actions.
109. I take much pride in being a man.
110. I am a loving and caring husband.
111. I am In awe of the person that I am and I am proud of the person I am becoming
112. My partner is my soul mate. We complement each other.
113. My body is healthy; my mind is brilliant; my soul is tranquil.

114. The world needs my uniqueness because everything about me is special
115. I am a loving and nurturing brother. I care for and dote on my sister.
116. I am a man who is confident and strong yet caring and corroborative.
117. I deserve to be employed and paid well for my time, efforts, and ideas.
118. I believe I can do anything in this life.
119. My obstacles are moving out of my way; my path is carved towards greatness.
120. I am a man who knows how to relax and have a good time.
121. I am a great protector of the people in my life and of my family.
122. I am great at my job and I am acknowledged for this
123. I am a man who laughs at himself with childish joy.
124. Many people look up to me and recognize my worth; I am admired.
125. I am a man who finds opportunities and advantages behind every door I open.
126. A river of compassion washes away my anger and replaces it with love.
127. My ability to conquer my challenges is limitless; my potential to succeed is infinite.
128. I am a prepared man who has a results-oriented daily plan.
129. I am a man with passions and I pursue them with intensity and fervor.
130. I am not consumed by work. I create time for my hobbies and activities I enjoy.
131. My mental and physical strength are incredibly strong.
132. I am a peaceful man who creates synergistic and positive relationships.
133. I am manly and perfectly enough.

134. Today, I am brimming with energy and overflowing with joy.
135. I have complete faith that everything is going to turn out perfectly I my favor
136. My subconscious properly prepares the subconscious of every other man I meet for positive interaction
137. I am powerful in so many ways and I celebrate this power daily
138. I am a man who is youthful and adventurous and spontaneous.
139. I am a vibrant powerhouse; I am indestructible.
140. No one negative is allowed to be in my life.
141. My life is just beginning.
142. When I speak to other men I focus on their interests not mine.
143. I am a man who takes direct action towards goals to build massive momentum.
144. Each day, I am closer to finding the perfect job for me.
145. I am grateful for everything in my life.
146. I follow my dreams as if my life depends on it, because it does.
147. I create harmony with other men through cooperative effort not competition.
148. My business is growing, expanding, and thriving.
149. I have made up me mind and decided that I'm going to relax and have fun with this day, no matter what the outcome may be
150. I am a responsible and trusting man who sees the good in others.
151. I encourage other men to talk about themselves and I listen intently when they do
152. Everywhere I go people are drawn to my dynamic masculine personality.
153. I possess the qualities needed to be extremely successful.

154. I am a strong man who is an outstanding and confident leader.
155. My nature is Divine; I am a spiritual being.
156. I am a great leader who can see the point of view of other men.
157. I accept, love, and appreciate myself, exactly as I am with no conditions.
158. I am worthy. I love and respect myself and always make life supporting loving choices in all areas
159. The perfect partner for me is coming into my life sooner than I expect.
160. I treat myself with kindness
161. Prosperity and masculinity are my birthrights and it shows through my actions.
162. I am sure of myself.
163. The tone of my masculine voice communicates strength and confidence.
164. I am supported, safe, and free to be myself
165. I make the choice to love and accept myself exactly as I am
166. I am at peace with all that has happened, is happening, and will happen.
167. I have a magnetic, warm, and masculine presence and handshake.
168. I am a man with enough time, energy, and wisdom to accomplish my desires.
169. My magnetism and masculine charm are noticed as soon as I walk into a room.
170. Today, I am ready for a healthy, loving relationship
171. I take great care to develop my personality.
172. When I speak with other men they notice how confident and fun I am.
173. I am a leader and influential man who gains respect through my actions.

174. I am a tower of strength, vitality, and masculinity and women notice it.
175. I wake up today with strength in my heart and clarity in my mind.
176. I express my honest and sincere appreciation for other men easily and often.
177. When I am around other men I feel content and strong.
178. I am conquering my illness; I am defeating it steadily each day.
179. I am a leader and I sincerely recognize the value in every other man I meet.
180. Every day, I learn and continue to grow into the best version of myself.
181. My personal experiences have made me the strong man I am today.
182. I am courageous and I stand up for myself.
183. I am a man who follows his gut instinct and I always find a reward.
184. I am a man who releases the need to be right all the time and to judge others.
185. I am a serious career person and I work hard to further my career.
186. I am confident about the way I look.
187. I am smart and witty and I am okay with myself
188. In my workplace where I lead, I get the best out of each employee.
189. My skills are unique and have enormous worth.
190. I love myself and the people around me.
191. I am a natural leader.

CHAPTER THIRTEEN

POSITIVE AFFIRMATIONS FOR TEENAGERS

1. I know it is okay not to have all the answers for my life right now, I take one day at a time.
2. All my school goals are being accomplished with ease.
3. I find it easy to be myself around new and old friends.
4. I am responsible teen. I own up to my actions
5. Spending time with my peers feels fun and invigorating.
6. I feel so great in my own skin.
7. I have the ability to choose any feeling I am feeling, therefore I always choose confidence.
8. I grow more confident from the challenges that life brings me.
9. I know that mom and dad want the best for me so I listen to what they have to say and respect them.
10. I tune out the voices of peer pressure and I listen to my parents because I know they want the best for me.
11. I have learned to stay calm in stressful situations.
12. I am so thankful for the ability to learn and grow from my teachers.
13. I sleep very soundly helping me have more energy in the day.
14. I am a genius and smarter than anyone I know.
15. Every new thing I try, I do really good at it.
16. I am not a social outcast
17. I feel great in who I am becoming.
18. I accomplish great things when I put my mind to it
19. I am blessed and God keeps me safe and secure.
20. I am super proud of myself.
21. I embrace my imperfections and grow from them.

22. I am really compassionate and passionate about the world
23. I am fearless
24. I easily let go of negative people in my life, they have no place in my life.
25. I am incredibly gifted, unique and special.
26. I am very determined.
27. I use my powerful ability to love for myself and give it to others as well.
28. I naturally find and embrace my talents and passions.
29. I have a really good attitude.
30. In school, I am a quick learner.
31. I am so creative and I get better every day
32. I have an awesome sense of humor and love to make my friends laugh.
33. I play so well with new and old friends.
34. I feel total relaxed when I go to parties.
35. I am a great friend. I have healthy that lasts a long time
36. I love eating health and exercising.
37. I love trying and learning new things in and out of school.
38. I create good habits in my life that will help propel me nicely into adulthood.
39. I love my family and love helping them with things.
40. I am learning a lot about myself right now and I keep doing so because it is so important to know thyself.
41. I am confident about myself and my abilities.
42. I choose how I feel and choose to feel loved and great all the time.
43. I have a retentive memory. I retain everything I study with ease.
44. I discover new talents that I have all the time.
45. There is nothing that I can't set my mind to and not achieve.
46. My dreams are possible to achieve.
47. I feel great and at ease eating in front of others.
48. I always do my best in everything I do

49. I feed my mind with positive content which transforms my mind and life for the better.
50. I am worthy of living my best life.
51. I am powerful kid
52. I naturally let go of relationships that are not supportive of me creating and keep high levels of self confidence.
53. I never try to act or be like anyone else because I love myself just the way I am.
54. I am appreciative to be at this young stage of life where there are so many possibilities.
55. I am very helpful around the house.
56. I am enough.
57. I am a great and valuable person with a lot to offer.
58. I am becoming a better me every single day.
59. I do my homework super fast right when I get home.
60. I choose my emotional state and therefore I always choose a state that makes me feel great about myself.
61. I am a great listener.
62. I can trust mom and dad with anything on my heart.
63. I feel like I am in a judge free zone when I am in social situations.
64. I am a fast learner, failing is a part of that process
65. I know that the more I like and accept myself, the more others will too.
66. I am so smart and intelligent.
67. I have all that it takes.
68. I love my life so much.
69. I feel so at ease in social situations.
70. I love being in social situations.
71. I can let go of worries I have anytime I want to. I have that power.
72. I attract other confident people into my life who I model and learn from which grows my level of confidence .

73. My courage overpowers any feeling of lack of self confidence.
74. I care about others and love to show my kindness.
75. I don't resist people trying to help me, I trust that they want what is best for me.
76. I am a very hard worker and always do my homework on time
77. I bless confident people because what I bless comes back to me.
78. I get better I school because I am a quick learner.
79. I am a natural at all the subjects and classes I take.
80. I love being myself and being around people who value the real me
81. My best self always comes out in social situations.
82. I am highly intelligent and bring a lot of value to my interactions.
83. I love being a kid
84. I make new friends so easily
85. People believe in me and think I am great.
86. I know I am loved by God.
87. I may not know what is best for me at all times, and I accept that and seek help when I need to do so.
88. I respect all my friends, teachers and family.
89. I am never a victim of my circumstances.
90. I am not afraid to try new things and challenge myself.
91. I am so thankful for my friends and family.
92. I let go of any anxiety and fear I have right now.
93. I know that honesty is always the best policy.
94. I am gifted and blessed and share it with the world.
95. All my problems have perfect solutions. I do not let worry consume me
96. I use my body to create a feel of confidence by standing tall and proud and opening myself up.
97. I have the right people to counsel me when I need it
98. I am contented with what I have and I am happier for it

99. I allow myself to learn great life lessons at this time of my life.
100. I wake up each day with energy and happiness.
101. I am a highly competent student.
102. I believe in myself.
103. I am always honest. Honest is the best policy.
104. I am safe in the here and now.
105. I am enough and I will not be made to feel less
106. I can share the truth with my parents and teachers about my life.
107. I naturally hang out with people who want the best for me and inspire me to grow and become more.
108. I can do anything I set my mind to.
109. I see all of the good things I have done in this life and it makes me feel great about myself.
110. I love myself.
111. I am so naturally gifted.
112. It feels great to be at ease whenever I am at a social gathering.
113. I believe in my capabilities.
114. My mind is strong and powerful.
115. I believe and trust myself.
116. I respect my teacher and love learning from him/her.
117. I allow myself to engage in my passions each day because it helps me live in the moment.
118. I love my friends and family and love to show them that I do.
119. I know mistakes only help me get better.
120. I am completely consumed and dedicated to my studies.
121. I always use my words to communicate during arguments.
122. I have no fear of speaking in public.
123. I do not hold grudges. I forgive people who are mean to me.
124. I accept myself completely.

125. I am confident enough to speak up for myself
126. I accept my body as it is changing and growing.
127. My teachers see the greatness in my that I may not even yet see.
128. Whether my parents at present or not, I try to adhere to the values they teach me
129. I have so much worth.
130. At home or at school, I feel safe and secure.
131. Confidence oozes out of me in social situations.
132. I am a knowledge seeker. I love learning new things in and out of school.
133. I trust my intuition to guide me in making good decisions.
134. I trust that I will do good in school and in life.
135. I am unique, truly one of a kind.
136. I have the best and most positive friends.
137. I already see myself graduating with honors and walking across the stage victorious.
138. I am always so happy.
139. I pay attention to the things I feed my mind with
140. I feel good about who I am and who I am becoming.
141. I allow myself to feel lost at times for I know I will find myself.
142. I feel so loved and protected by my family.
143. People always tend to really like me.
144. I am making deliberate choices about my future
145. I find it easy to sink into very good study sessions.
146. I am a wise teen
147. I always find myself not even thinking about my social anxiety.
148. In am divinely protected from any form of abuse
149. I love meeting new people.
150. I am a happy and generous person and people do not take advantage of that
151. I strive for purpose and progress, not perfection.

152. I am a child of excellence
153. I give myself permission to only study things that bring me happiness and fulfillment
154. Even though I am young, I still am grateful for each day for I know life is short.
155. I choose good and healthy foods because I love my body.
156. My mind always chooses positive and uplifting thoughts that help me feel great about myself.
157. I love hanging out with my family and sharing my love with them.
158. My breath is perfectly controlled when I am social situations.
159. Everything will be okay
160. I am enough.
161. Failure is not the end of the road. I know I can always do better next time.
162. I don't judge myself, I love myself.
163. I feel very beautiful/handsome at all times.
164. I love exercising my body and love the way I feel because of it.
165. I naturally see myself doing things in life with grace and perfection, hence I go into these situations feeling very confident.
166. When people say negative things to me, I don't care because I love and respect myself.
167. I feel like a natural talking to people in social situations.
168. I can make really good choices, and if I make a poor choice, I have the right support system to help me through it.
169. I am thankful that I have such a great teacher.
170. It is safe for me to open up in front of people.
171. I am whole, perfect and complete.
172. The universe supports and wants to help me feel the most confident.

173. I am not confined by fear as I always break through my fears.
174. I am proud of myself and the accomplishments I have made so far
175. I come to class with a wide open growth mindset.
176. I am not easily distracted as I have really good focusing skills.
177. Everything I do makes me feel even more proud of myself.
178. Life is an adventure do me because I am brave and confident.
179. I am very responsible. I carry out my chores diligently
180. I ace my tests with ease.
181. The mistakes I make do not define me. I learn from all of my mistakes.
182. I let go of all my feelings of low self-esteem, right now.
183. I am in charge of my emotions, no one else.
184. I am in my element in social situations.
185. I enjoy learning because I grow when I do
186. There are so many opportunities for me in life and I embrace them all
187. It feels great to be a child of God.
188. I choose to let my life overflow with joy and self confidence.
189. I see life as a classroom which helps me crush my school goals.
190. I make easy connections with the subjects I am studying help me memorize and learn better.
191. I am making a positive impact in this generation

CHAPTER FOURTEEN

POSITIVE AFFIRMATIONS FOR PREGNANCY

1. My birth is going to be perfect and quick.
2. I am committed to consciously raising this child. All the unconscious generational negativity stops with me
3. Birth is safe for me and my baby.
4. I choose to enjoy every second in this journey of pregnancy, even in difficult days.
5. My baby loves me.
6. I welcome the challenge of motherhood with grace, gratitude, and a warm heart filled with love.
7. I have the right support system to help me through this pregnancy and beyond
8. I accept my labor and birth.
9. I am a strong woman.
10. My husband/boyfriend and I will become deeply connected during and after the birthing process.
11. I assertively use my voice to express what I want and need and to say no when I'm uncomfortable.
12. My baby feels my love.
13. I educate myself to make the best possible decisions for my pregnancy and my baby's birth.
14. I am the best parent for my baby.
15. The world welcomes my baby into this world with love and open arms.
16. I have no fear about the birthing process, I let go of it now.
17. I feel blessed, privileged, and favored to carry my baby inside of me.

18. I am bringing a perfectly healthy, whole, and strong child into this world.
19. I love my baby even though we are yet to meet
20. I believe in myself and my natural ability to give birth easily, peacefully, and in comfort.
21. I know how to take care of myself in pregnancy.
22. My baby loves me fully and completely.
23. My body knows exactly how to care for my growing baby.
24. My baby is in the perfect position to come to the world efficiently and smoothly.
25. I love and approve of myself and I welcome, honor, and embrace the changes in my beautiful pregnant body as it shifts to accommodate my baby.
26. I am surrounded by those who love and respect me.
27. I was divinely chosen and called to be the mother of this child and I am good enough to care for her/him
28. I will be ready and prepared for a safe, beautiful, and effortless birthing experience.
29. My love and connection with this child within me humbles me every day. I am blessed and I know it.
30. My baby cannot wait to get to this world!
31. My body is accepting my baby and my pregnancy will end with the safe birth of a healthy baby.
32. As the motherhood chapter of my life begins, I am ready to make it a beautiful chapter in my life.
33. My pregnant body is beautiful.
34. I am in perfect health. My baby is in perfect health. This pregnancy comes to a perfect end.
35. I rely on millennia of maternal instincts embedded in me. I know how to take care of my baby.
36. Breathing in, I know I am a great mother. Breathing out, I am a great mother
37. My body knows how to give birth.

38. I cherish and celebrate the gift of pregnancy, life, and motherhood.
39. The concept of labor doesn't scare me as I know that contractions help to bring my baby.
40. I deeply trust my instincts and my body, and I trust I am capable of safely delivering my baby.
41. I have an amazing support system! When I ask for help, I receive help.
42. My baby will be born at the perfect time.
43. I allow myself to see the beauty and joy in this process, to enjoy this precious time with my baby, and to be empowered by all it brings.
44. I visualize myself after a perfect delivery. I am at home loving and playing with my beautiful baby.
45. I have a close bond with my baby. My relationships with my baby is so strong.
46. My doctor and I are on the same page. We are partners in delivering a healthy, happy baby.
47. My baby knows the true birthday.
48. I trust my body to make the labor process as easy and effective as possible.
49. I am remaining alert, in tune, and aware of my needs and I intuitively know the needs of my baby.
50. I protect myself and my baby by allowing only positive thoughts and words about pregnancy and childbirth.
51. How my child is born is solely my choice and I choose natural birth!
52. I will make plenty of breast milk for my baby.
53. This pregnancy is not a complicated one
54. My body knows when to give birth.
55. My baby is loved and she senses my love as our bond and connection grows stronger every day.
56. I am proud myself for the contribution of carrying, nurturing, and sustaining a life within me.

57. I feel powerful and healthy during the birthing process.
58. My body was made to nurture a baby.
59. I am happy and excited about my pregnancy and I'm looking forward to a calm, quiet, and beautiful birth.
60. My neuro-muscular system is working in perfect harmony during my delivery.
61. I choose the see the beauty in this whole process of bringing a new life into the world.
62. My midwife is a beautiful friend and wise counsel throughout my pregnancy. I am lucky to have her
63. I am deserving of an easy and uncomplicated pregnancy.
64. My pregnancy is a gift.
65. I am calm, cool, and confident throughout my pregnancy. This is the most beautiful nine months of my life
66. My baby is developing normally and will be born healthy, whole, safe, and at the perfect time.
67. My growing body is beautiful because of its power.
68. I know this is the right time for my baby to come to the world and bless our family.
69. My baby is growing just as she/he should.
70. My most important job in pregnancy and childbirth is to simply relax, stay centered, serene, and balanced, and to allow my baby's birth to happen.
71. I have built a harmonious union with my doctor/midwife/doula.
72. Despite difficulties, I remain energized, strong and healthy.
73. I am an amazing mother about to have an amazing baby
74. I am well cared for by myself and my loved ones.
75. My pregnancy is perfect. I am delivering a happy, healthy baby
76. My body accepts and protects this baby.
77. I am a strong women perfectly capable of a healthy and perfect birth.
78. Without any doubt, I believe that I am a great mother

79. My body was designed to nourish, protect, and grow my baby in my belly.
80. I am excited about my journey
81. I make the best decisions for myself and my baby.
82. I am strong and healthy and sailing right through this pregnancy.
83. I feel confident that every change my body goes through is for my baby's good.
84. I conceived a beautiful baby and I am delivering a beautiful child.
85. Today, I declare that my womb is functioning optimally.
86. My baby is receiving all the nourishment and nurturance that it needs.
87. My baby and I are working together to prepare for her birth and we are both grateful for this powerful experience.
88. I declare that I am healthy; my body is healthy.
89. My baby is so special to me and so is my body.
90. With each contraction I feel stronger and more powerful.
91. I am having fun with my pregnancy. I enjoy each week. I savor each milestone.
92. I am a great mother. My new baby is lucky to have me
93. My body is a relaxed and a warm home for my growing baby.
94. I will listen to my intuition and what it is telling me to make the process more natural and easy.
95. Today, I am feeling energized.
96. My body is a loving, safe home for my growing bundle of joy.
97. As my healthy baby grows within me, I am more attuned than ever to the perfect rhythms of nature and my body.
98. I trust that my body knows exactly what it is doing.
99. My baby knows how and when to be born and I patiently await for her arrival.
100. I will be a great mother.
101. My body was made for this experience

102. My life will soon be better because my baby will be in it.
103. I choose to be happy for me and my baby.
104. I crave healthy nutrition throughout this pregnancy
105. I am going to be perfectly relaxed during the birthing process.
106. I crave nutritious foods and I enjoy every meal that I share with my baby
107. I transcend all pain during the birthing process.
108. My womb is full of love.
109. I trust my body knows how to safely guide my baby out of the womb and into my arms.
110. My body is strong and capable.
111. My partner is uniquely equipped to care for me and the baby
112. There may be difficult days during this pregnancy, but I am strong, I am determined, and I am resilient.
113. I take deep breaths and feel the presence of my baby inside my body.
114. I am forming plenty of milk for my baby and I appreciate all the work from my breasts.
115. From conception to birth, I am having a wonderful experience
116. I release the discomfort of pregnancy, I let go of the worry, tension and the fear of birth and I am focused on the joy of meeting my child.
117. I release all my fears and trust that I am ready for this
118. Giving birth is normal and natural and my baby and I will be healthy and happy when it is over.
119. I am mentally, financially, emotionally and spiritually equipped for this pregnancy
120. I envelope myself in a warm and positive blanket that comforts and nurtures the life growing inside of me
121. An amazing mother lives within me. That mother is born along with my baby.

122. No Matter the sex of the baby, my baby is perfect.
123. I am absolutely committed to providing my child with a safe and happy home environment.
124. I am a perfectly functional engine for the creation of life
125. I will be patient and courage throughout the entire birthing process.
126. My uterus is full of life-giving energy.
127. I am attentive to this experience. I am committed to optimal nutrition, exercise and rest.
128. My body is powerful and full of light
129. I was made to be a mother. I trust my body.
130. It's so exciting to know that a new life is growing inside me.
131. I love my pregnant body- it is radiant, beautiful, and blissful because it is equipped everything I need to take care of my baby.
132. My pregnancy scars tell a story of my journey to creating life
133. I see myself right in the here and now, holding my beautiful baby in my arms. We are both happy, healthy and better yet intimately connected.
134. I welcome every experience on this journey to motherhood
135. I will be active to ensure a great delivery and a healthy baby.
136. Each pregnancy is a unique and beautiful experience. I am consciously enjoying this unique journey
137. Every kick is a reminder of a developing blessing inside of me.
138. A warm feeling fills me as I think of the amazing miracle forming inside my body.
139. I choose to experience the beauty of a natural birth and so that IS what I will experience
140. Just breathe and know that everything will be okay.

141. I take a deep breath and I smile every time I think of my pregnancy
142. The bond between me and my baby is inseparable.
143. There's life inside of me that I will care for the rest of my life.
144. I am not afraid of labor. I feel closer and closer to my baby with each contraction.
145. I will think positively, for everything will be fine and my baby is going to be fine.
146. My baby knows the love I have and is feeling this inside its entire body.
147. All the parts of my body are working together in harmony for a healthy, smooth and happy pregnancy.
148. There's beauty in the growth of my belly and the rest of my body.
149. My whole family is going to be deeply and intimately connected after our birth.
150. I caress my tummy and sense my baby enjoying this time inside my womb.
151. My choices throughout this pregnancy are based on facts not fear
152. My body is accepting this baby and will protect it.
153. On this journey to birthing, I accept the help of others.
154. Any day now, my life will change for the better with you in it.
155. My body is beautifully nourishing the child I carry. My child is perfectly healthy.
156. My body is perfectly qualified for this journey
157. I consult with my doctor, but I listen to my body and my heart when deciding how I will give birth.
158. I am enjoying my pregnancy one butterfly flutter at a time.
159. I am blessed and favored to be able to have this baby inside of me.
160. I am envisioning a healthy delivery of a healthy baby.

161. I let go of all worries, pre-birth, during birth and post-birth.
162. I am capable of delivering this baby.
163. I share affirming, warm and loving words with my baby.
164. My baby is safe and forming perfectly.
165. I will make the right decisions for my baby.
166. An amazing mother lives within me and will be born along with my amazing baby.
167. This is a great time. This is a miraculous experience. I'm excited to become a mom.
168. My love for you will grow every day just like you will.
169. My baby's head fits snugly into my pelvis.
170. I trust my body to help guide my baby into this world, into my arms.
171. I feel connected to my baby and my baby feels connected to me.
172. I am strong and ready to give birth to a beautiful healthy baby.
173. My baby is developing into a strong, happy and secure person.
174. My happiness is within my womb and will be here in 9 months.
175. I can endure all and will endure all that comes my way.
176. I look forward to developing a loving relationship with my baby and watching him/her grow to be a successful and happy adult.
177. I will cherish every little toe, finger, bone, face expression, and more.
178. As I care for myself well, I care for my baby well.
179. My soul loves you baby.
180. My baby senses the peace I feel.
181. I maintain peace go myself and my baby. I am the peacekeeper of my life.
182. My baby will find the perfect position for birth.
183. Every week is a step closer to meeting my bundle of joy.

184. I speak loving words to my child and I speak loving words to myself.
185. I am a highly-capable mother-to-be! If there are hard decisions to make, I can and I will make them
186. Everything I need to take care of this baby is already within me.
187. My morning sickness is the overwhelming emotions of happiness my baby has because I am their mother.
188. I am good enough to be the mother this child needs and care for this child within me.
189. The foods I eat are nourishing my child's body.
190. I am a good mother.
191. I conceived this baby in love. I am delivering this baby in love. I will raise this baby with love.
192. I cannot wait to bond with my little one.
193. My body is perfectly capable of nourishing the life within

CHAPTER FIFTEEN

POSITIVE AFFIRMATIONS FOR TOUGH TIMES

1. Regardless of the challenge, I'm creating value in the world through my business.
2. Challenges are opportunities to learn and grow.
3. My bills are paid and I will live freely. I refuse to worry
4. I can get through anything in my life.
5. I will learn what I need to from today which will make me a stronger person.
6. When I have done all I know how to do, I choose to let my mind rest.
7. I know when to persevere along a path and when to let go and change course.
8. Whatever I am going through is guiding me to where I want to go.
9. I create a joyful, peaceful world to live in regardless of the challenges
10. The challenges I face give me energy and purpose.
11. Though these times are difficult, they are only a short phase of life.
12. This business is growing at the right speed for it to become successful.
13. I easily flow with the changes I experience
14. I am safe and secure no matter what.
15. Hard times do not get the best of me.
16. I have the strength and courage to get through any situation.
17. I welcome fear as a sign to be careful, but choose to let go of it when it no longer serves me.

18. My commitment to showing up tomorrow overshadows the mistakes I have made.
19. There are no problems, only challenges.
20. When I have a crisis at work, I remind myself that I earn plenty of money and love what I do.
21. Today, money comes to me effortlessly.
22. I let go of any stress and anxiety from today.
23. I welcome challenges into my life.
24. I can get through anything.
25. I have the ability to overcome any obstacle
26. I know that life is not meant to be easy so I brace myself for the seasons
27. Today may be tough, but tomorrow is a brand new day.
28. I can and will survive anything life throws at me.
29. I am doing what I can with the knowledge and skills I have to survive this.
30. Nothing lasts forever. This experience too will pass
31. I am worthy of love and my life is meaningful despite my losses.
32. I can get through anything.
33. My income is constantly growing. I am not worried
34. I am ready to become the best version of myself.
35. I am getting stronger everyday.
36. I don't have to go this road alone. I have, or can find, people in my life and examples to support and inspire me.
37. I welcome challenges into my life.
38. When circumstances change, I will feel all the more grateful for what I have.
39. I am holding on in the dark to what I know to be true in the light, in better times.
40. I boldly face my fears as courage does not mean having no fear of danger, but facing the danger despite that fear
41. I can solve any problem.

42. Life's problems are not solved by perfect people, but by those who show up. I am someone who shows up.
43. I will not let fear take control of me.
44. I don't have to have this all solved today.
45. I attract financial abundance into my life.
46. I am flexible and can adapt when life doesn't go according to plan.
47. I am doing the best I can, and thus choose to release myself from guilt and shame.
48. Life is full of constant change. My pain, though very real, will not be as acute forever.
49. I am slowly becoming the kind of person who can survive this storm.
50. This is just one chapter in my life's story.
51. I am protected; I am safe
52. The freedom that I gain from running my own business is my biggest reward.
53. There is a huge demand for my particular skills and abilities. I will not be frustrated
54. I am not a burden on anyone as I earn good money and enjoy what I do
55. I know that I deserve love and I accept it even now
56. I am a strong and capable person.
57. I laugh at life and choose not to be offended by anyone or anything
58. My ability to achieve greatness within this challenge is limitless.
59. I am not alone. I make friends easily wherever I go
60. I am not carrying emotional baggage. I release old hurt, resentment and anger easily
61. I forgive myself for past failures.
62. No matter what happens, I am gentle kind and patient with myself
63. I go with the flow, my life is easy and filled with joy

64. The present challenges cannot define me. The past has no power of me
65. Breathing in I am calm. Breathing out I smile. I remain calm
66. Helping others get what they want is the first step in getting what I want.
67. I release all negative emotions from the day.
68. My family's needs are met and more through the work that I'm doing.
69. I am not deterred by the troubles confronting me. My dreams for my business align with my core values in life.
70. On this journey, I trust myself and I trust life
71. No matter what I see in the news, I am safe wherever I turn
72. My success is inevitable if I keep working hard to reach my goals.
73. I am thankful to others who have helped me. I am thankful to myself.
74. The universe sends positive vibes my way
75. My passions sustain me as I'm doing what I love and my income is growing every day.
76. I am a strong person.
77. Today I'm creating opportunities to grow myself and my business. Nothing can hold me down
78. Despite the negative voices, what I'm doing is making a difference in the world.
79. Challenges in business cannot stop me. I am a natural entrepreneur. This is my calling in life.
80. I am filled with joy and ease right now.
81. I am not exhausting myself. The value-generating aspects of my business are where I put my effort.
82. Where others see a challenge, I see new opportunities.
83. I will be proactive in discovering obstacles to my accomplishments.
84. I couple courage and action with high hopes to enjoy the best life possible.

85. I know everything works out for me in the end.
86. I know that my situation right now is temporary and it is only getting better every day.
87. I release all negativity from my life.
88. I am not a failure, but a survivor. I am daily in the process of surviving.
89. I am surrounded by hopeful and positive people.
90. I completely surrender and let go of any illusion about control
91. I desire to learn new things.
92. There is a a plan for my life and this is just something I need to overcome.
93. I can, I will, I must overcome this.
94. I laugh at my feelings of depression which makes them dissipate.
95. I am constantly improving.
96. I know that I will become a stronger version of myself for what I am going through.
97. Time is my friend. I finish all the tasks I need to finish.
98. I choose to completely transcend these feelings of depression.
99. Answers about how to feel better come to me with ease.
100. I am not the only one to have faced this sort of trauma, and I will not be the last.
101. I believe in myself and love myself.
102. This is not the life that is designed for me.
103. I am standing up inside myself for myself
104. I feel heavy feelings lifting.
105. My mind and body feel clear and positive.
106. I choose to be easy on myself.
107. The outer world cannot shake my inner peace. I trust that all is well and everything is working out for my highest and greatest good.
108. I am constantly finding new activities that help me feel positive and motivated.
109. I know that all my wishes are being fulfilled.

110. People support me on my journey and lift up my spirits because they love me.
111. My life gets better everyday
112. I have no fear of asking loved ones to support and help me along my journey.
113. My challenges are real, but I can stay positive through them.
114. God is lifting my depression.
115. Mindfulness will help me get the most from my time.
116. I decide that I can heal myself completely.
117. I take responsibility for my successes and my failures.
118. Everything is temporary. Success is temporary. Failure is temporary.
119. Everything that happens to me is another opportunity to choose love.
120. This too shall pass.
121. No fear can scare me: I am bold!
122. I naturally use my body to counteract feelings of depression. I maintain strong stances that help me feel happy and confident.
123. I will not be discouraged. This is my calling in life.
124. No matter what, I love working. It energizes me and brings me focus.
125. No matter the challenges I face, I remain strong, calm and at peace!
126. I always remain strong
127. I always remain bold
128. andI always remain determined and with faith in my heart!
129. I am a strong person and I go on. I always go on!
130. My life is a bold life!
131. I naturally seek growth and personal development for it makes me feel better and more positive.
132. The success that I want is the natural end of the work that I'm doing.

133. I am the most powerful person I know and nothing slows me down
134. Each minute of my life, I am bold
135. All my wants and needs are being fulfilled by the universe.
136. My passion and my purpose drive me through challenges and towards success.
137. I naturally let go of people aren't contributing to the creation of positive mental health for me.
138. My experiences are bold experiences
139. I feel more and more positive each day.
140. I am a brave person
141. I naturally let go of all negative thoughts that are contributing to my depression.
142. In this economy, my business makes me stronger and happier.
143. There is nothing that I can conceive that I cannot achieve.
144. I have great powers within me
145. I naturally think positive, empowering and uplifting thoughts.
146. I am stronger. I can move mountains.
147. I have the ability to manifest my goals and dreams whenever I choose.
148. I know how to remain bold and unshakable!
149. I am thankful for the lessons life has taught me for they have made me stronger.
150. What I speak comes into fruition into my life, therefore I only speak positively.
151. No situation can come on my way
152. I am transforming my life for the better in every area of my life.
153. My life is made for joy. I will live with exuberance.
154. I completely forgive and love myself in the here and now.
155. I overcome all obstacles

156. I know that I am guided in this life and have faith my life will turn out perfectly.
157. There is nothing I cannot overcome.
158. I easily let go of people who are negative and not supportive.
159. I am not forgotten. My energy attracts the customers and clients that I need to be successful.
160. I have so much value to add and give to the world.
161. I naturally attract more success and happiness every day.
162. I am not dependent on anyone else. But I accept help when it is offered
163. I have hope for a better future.
164. I have what it takes to make my dreams come true.
165. I am likeable and positive.
166. The comeback is always greater than the set back.
167. I am aware that I am the creator of my existence.
168. I know that no challenges is too big for me to take on and triumph over.
169. I always have so much hope.
170. I don't listen or pay attention to negative people and what they say.
171. I feel so positive about the direction my life is going.
172. I follow through and persevere towards my dreams no matter what.
173. I am thankful for the ability to have hope.
174. I let go of all the worries I have for it drains me of vital energy.
175. I have the courage to keep moving forward.
176. I love how my passions give me hope for a better future.
177. I am decisive and always make excellent decisions in these times
178. I have more strength that I know.
179. I attract people into my life that are positive and uplifting.
180. I seek happiness from within.

181. I do not define myself by my diagnosis, it is just an opinion.
182. I feel completely at ease with the world.
183. I feel great in my own skin.
184. I create positive changes in my life with ease.
185. I choose to replace negative thoughts with positive thoughts with ease.
186. I love who I am, completely.
187. Hope is always a solution to all my problems.
188. I have a growth mindset.
189. I am completely renewed with high levels of hope each day.
190. I admit my true feelings. This is not a weakness, it is a strength that simply hasn't been revealed to me yet.
191. I will not be crushed by my circumstances

CHAPTER SIXTEEN

POSITIVE AFFIRMATIONS FOR WEIGHT LOSS

1. I believe I can lose weight
2. My health is the most important thing to me
3. I am avoiding excessive carbs
4. I am happy and grateful to have lost ____ pounds
5. There is no need for rich or sugary foods
6. I have the power to control my weight through healthy eating and exercise
7. My body is a temple. I will keep my temple clean
8. I can go with the flow.
9. My body is my best friend.
10. When I eat well, exercise and get enough sleep, I am investing in myself.
11. I am proud of all my body does for me, every single day.
12. I listen to what my body needs.
13. I do not compare my body to other peoples' bodies.
14. I love what my body is capable of doing now and in the future.
15. I am thankful that my body is both beautiful and strong.
16. I use my body with love, pride and care.
17. I am allowed to have bad days.
18. I am brave to endure days like today.
19. I am patient with and kind to myself.
20. Tomorrow is more than another day; it's another chance to shine.
21. I look forward to feeling better about things again.
22. Life is tough sometimes, but so am I.

23. I am a survivor and that makes me proud of myself.
24. On hard days like this, I love myself more than ever.
25. My bad days and unhappy moments will always pass.
26. I can see the end of this hard time, and I move towards it with every breath I take.
27. I deserve to feel good about myself right now.
28. This positive energy is of my own creating.
29. I am excited by and for life.
30. I savor feeling good about myself.
31. It is important that I take a moment to cherish feeling at peace with myself.
32. These good days feed my soul and help me prepare for harder times.
33. I celebrate myself and what I have achieved today, and every day.
34. The future is bright, and so is the light shining inside me.
35. I aim to share with others the positivity and love I feel for life.
36. I smile with confidence in myself and in the future.
37. I do not have to change for anybody.
38. There is nobody else in the world like me. That is my magic.
39. I am not afraid to be different.
40. I go to bed early so I can wake up rested and strong.
41. I attract nature's limitless abilities to help me alter my current body weight
42. My body can heal and reach new goals, thanks to nature.
43. My body and mind are being restored as excessive and a toxic mindset exits it.
44. I acknowledge that nature has a nutritious healing strength that fills my body and soul.
45. The foods nature provides are transforming my body and making me whole.
46. I recognize that each day in nature is a gift from the universe and try to spend time outdoors.
47. I eat a balanced diet, and exercise daily.

48. I embrace the energy food provides me each day.
49. I completely understand that unhealthy foods do not help me lose weight, so I eat only healthy, nutritious foods.
50. The sounds, smells, and visual aspects of nature have powers that revitalize and promotes health and I am drawn to them.
51. Healing is happening in both my body and mind.
52. I no longer feel the urge to stuff my body with unhealthy foods, and I can easily resist temptations.
53. I am the best version of myself, and I am working hard to become even better. I will lose weight because I want to, and I have the power to do this.
54. I manage stress by doing things that are healthy but effective like taking a warm bath or watching a funny movie.
55. I feel excitement when life brings challenges to me, and I gladly accept them without any guilt or anxiety.
56. I enjoy life by staying fit and maintaining my ideal weight.
57. Being myself is good and rewarding, and I always perceive challenges as opportunities to prove my abilities.
58. I have an appreciation for the great outdoors. This helps my body connect with nature so it can transform.
59. I understand my goals and let go of any negative thought patterns that discourage me from attaining them.
60. Every time I inhale, confidence fills my entire being and every time I exhale, all guilt and shyness get washed away.
61. I always chew my food properly so that my body can digest it and take out the nutrients
62. I am letting go of any guilt I hold around food.
63. I treasure my health and well-being. With a strong body and sound mind, I can take on challenges and fulfill my goals.
64. I have the right mindset. I am a focused person, and I will not quit doing anything when I feel challenged or wronged.
65. I know that I need to lose weight.
66. I acknowledge both my qualities and defects, and I always strive to improve.

67. I set myself free from all the guilt I carry around the food I chose in the past.
68. I choose to accept myself exactly the way I am, and be happy with my life.
69. I am closer and closer to my ideal weight with each and every day.
70. I have a strong urge to eat only healthy foods, and let go of any processed foods.
71. Every day is a new day to begin on a positive and stable foot.
72. I am intensely driven toward achieving my weight loss goal.
73. I believe in my ability to love and accept myself for who I am.
74. I believe in my ability to change my habits and create new, positive ones.
75. I love and embrace the weight loss journey, enjoying every single step of the way.
76. It is perfectly clear to me how all the positives about weight loss outweigh the negative.
77. I dwell on all the long term positive effects that my weight loss will bring me, and it inspires me
78. Every cell in my body is healthy and fit, and so am I.
79. I burn fat with ease.
80. I pay no attention to people telling me my goals aren't possible.
81. My weight goals are achievable because I invoke the power of nature.
82. I always envision myself at my ideal weight.
83. I love the idea of me being at maintaining my perfect body weight with ease.
84. My health is improving more and more every day, and so is my body.
85. I am arriving closer and closer each day to my perfect weight.

86. I feel stronger knowing nature's nutrients are working on my system and mind. I trust in their power to make a difference in my physical condition.
87. All the weight I lose, I lose permanently.
88. I am naturally raising the standard on myself and my health.
89. I can do this, I am doing this, my body is losing weight right now.
90. I give thanks for having a body that is capable of exercising and effectively losing weight.
91. I naturally eat in perfect and proper proportions.
92. Today, I recognize the healing power of nature in my life and feel grateful for this wonderful gift.
93. I easily work my workouts and exercise around my work and life schedule.
94. Every day I am exercising and taking care of my body.
95. I listen to my body when it tells me I need to eat, I do not eat out of boredom.
96. I am so happy and grateful now that I weigh _____ kilograms/pounds.
97. I am fully committed to getting down to my ideal body weight.
98. Nature is activating my body's self-repair mechanisms, so my weight loss goals are easier to achieve.
99. Not only is my health improving, but so is my entire life. And it feels great!
100. I am in complete control of my weight.
101. I am mastering my weight loss and health more and more each day.
102. Weight loss is as easy and natural for me as breathing in and out.
103. I love setting new goals for myself that keep me inspired and motivated to keep going with my weight loss.
104. My body is repairing and rebuilding itself because I embrace the naturally healthy things and this is helping.

105. I am being cleansed and unburdened by nature.
106. I am grateful for this new lifestyle change and love losing weight.
107. My focus and drive never wavers on my weight loss journey.
108. I accept my body exactly the way it is and I constantly work on improving it.
109. I belief in my abilities and know I have what it takes to transform my body and mind.
110. I see food as fuel, not as something to suppress emotions with.
111. I love the journey of health and commit to a lifestyle change, not just a diet plan. It is who I am now and forever.
112. I am closer and closer to my ideal weight with each and every day.
113. I easily let go of relationships that don't benefit my weight loss and health.
114. My metabolism is high and effective at burning fat and helping with weight loss.
115. I feel my desire for unhealthy fat-rich foods dissolving.
116. I enjoy eating healthy foods.
117. I have all the mental and physical power needed for effective and long lasting weight loss.
118. My fat loss is progressing each day, and progress feels so great
119. I feel my body losing weight in every single moment of the day till I hit my goals.
120. I am so thankful that there are so many tools and tips that I can use to get me fit for life.
121. I am becoming more physically active each day.
122. It is safe for me to change my body.
123. I inspire people with my dedication and commitment to fitness and weight loss.

124. Eating healthy foods helps my body get all of the nutrients it needs to be in best shape.
125. Everyone is different and I don't hold any expectations to my weight loss, only that it is and will keep happening.
126. I make choices with ease that support my weight loss journey.
127. I appreciate every single thing I have in my life, and I live in absolute joy.
128. My cardiovascular system is running perfectly, helping me reach my weight loss goals with ease.
129. I commit to loving myself throughout this entire journey.
130. I am capable of achieving my weight loss goals, and I will not let anything stay in my way until then.
131. I am literally watching fat melt of my body, more and more by the day.
132. I am craving healthy and whole foods more and more each day.
133. The whole universe conspires to help me with my weight loss and fat loss.
134. All my feelings and emotions are predicated around my weight loss.
135. I am attaining and maintaining my desired weight.
136. I sink into deep states of sleep and relaxation, helping my body recover perfectly each day.
137. Everything I eat heals and nourishes my body, which helps me reach the ideal weight.
138. My heart and soul is so passionate and driven toward achieving my weight loss goals.
139. I love going to the gym and eating healthy.
140. My body is my temple, and I attentively take care of it every day by eating only healthy foods that heal and nourish me.
141. Each and every cell in me feels healthy and vibrant.

142. I accept myself the way I am, and I am getting better and better in everything I do.
143. Being alive makes me a happy person.
144. I replace "I must," "I have to" and "I should" with "I choose."
145. I am true to my wonderful self.
146. I am loved for who I am right now.
147. In the future, all will be well with my beautiful soul.
148. I trust that I am strong enough to face whatever the future brings.
149. I commit to a new lifestyle that is beneficial not only for weight loss but for higher self confidence and self esteem.
150. I inhale self-confidence and exhale fear and anxiety.
151. I am perfectly full and satisfied with the perfect amount of food I need for fat loss
152. I am grateful to my body for all the things it does for me.
153. I listen to what my body tells me it needs.
154. All the people around me are in complete support of my weight loss.
155. I am aware that my metabolism is working in my advantage by helping me in gaining my optimal weight.
156. I love my body completely right, which helps me in my journey of losing weight.
157. I am fit and confident in my own body. tell my body and mind what to do. Not the other way around.
158. Meeting new people is easy. I can creative supportive relationships and make new friends without feeling anxious.
159. I prioritize working for progress and not perfection.
160. I can trust myself to go through with my weight loss plans
161. My mind is filled with positive thoughts
162. I set realistic but challenging goals for myself that inspire me to lose weight and feel great.
163. I naturally read and watching content that helps me gain knowledge and ideas for effective weight loss.

164. I have the power to easily control my weight through a combination of healthy eating and exercising.
165. Working out comes natural to me.
166. I trust myself, and I have the confidence that I am a worthy person everyone respects.
167. I trust myself fully and completely to make the right choices that create great weight loss.
168. My thoughts are constantly positive and revolve around positive images of me being fit and healthy.
169. I share with people my insights and tips for weight loss as I know they reinforce my new beliefs.
170. It matters little what other people say. What really matters to me is how I react and what I believe in.
171. I am kind, loving, compassionate, and I truly care for the people around.
172. I breathe in relaxation and breathe out stress.
173. I have all that it takes to lose weight and achieve my ideal body weight.
174. I am a confident person who is respected by everyone around.
175. I am a unique and worthy person, and I deserve everyone's respect.
176. I am enthusiastic and energetic, and confidence is an important part of my nature.
177. I respect myself, and so do others around me.
178. I accept myself, and I love myself for who I am.
179. I trust and believe in myself, and I let go of the negative.
180. I thrive on my absolute self-confidence. My body is beautiful, and I enjoy every single thing about it.
181. I deserve all that is good in this world. I release any need for suffering, and I can feel happiness, confidence and love getting into my body, mind, and soul.
182. I never compare myself to others, as I understand my uniqueness.

183. I have integrity, as I am a reliable person and I always do exactly what I say.
184. I am healthy, well-groomed, and good-looking, and I acknowledge both my inner and outer beauty.
185. Every time I inhale, fresh energy fills my entire being and every time I exhale, all toxins and body fat leave my body.
186. Change is inevitable and I accept it wholeheartedly.
187. I am a person who easily accepts new challenges.
188. I deserve good things in my future.
189. I look forward to living tomorrow, and tomorrow's tomorrow.
190. My metabolism rate is at its optimum level, and this helps me reach my ideal body weight.
191. Even in my dreams, ideas and inspiration come to me about weight loss.
192. Sometimes I don't know where I'm going, but I will find my way. And it will be fabulous.

CHAPTER SEVENTEEN

POSITIVE AFFIRMATIONS FOR MANIFESTING DESIRES

1. The Universe always has my back.
2. Opportunities arrive at the right time in the right place
3. Whatever I can conceive, I believe
4. Everything works out perfectly for me. I am creating my dream life.
5. I have a powerful and natural ability to visualize things that I desire
6. Something wonderful is about to happen to me
7. I listen deeply to the goals and dreams that are whispering to me now
8. Miracles manifest everyday in wondrous ways
9. It is ok for me to have everything I want. Every day I move towards having everything I want.
10. I live in the house of my dreams; in tranquil surroundings filled with love, a blessed family and happy kids
11. I am a master of converting the energy of my dreams into fuel for powerful action
12. Whenever I breathe, I inhale health and exhale misery. I attract a wonderful life.
13. I am worthy of receiving my yes. I now release everything that is not serving my highest purpose.
14. I am worthy enough to follow my greatest dreams and manifest my deepest desires
15. I always think about the other person first. Hence, my relationships are safe and secure.
16. If I see it in my mind, I am going to hold it in my hand.

17. I am worthy of love, abundance, success, happiness and fulfillment.
18. I now release any fears or limiting beliefs I may have about achieving my yes.
19. There is no place for negative self-talk in my life. I am completely and utterly in love with myself.
20. Always possibility, never lack
21. My higher self rules over my ego.
22. I am creating my dream life, and everything works out perfectly for me
23. My inner home is a peaceful retreat, a storehouse of practical wisdom.
24. I am worthy enough to follow my dreams and manifest my desires.
25. I effortlessly and frequently visualize living my life exactly as I desire
26. I use visualization to reprogram my subconscious
27. Increasingly confident in my ability to create the life I desire.
28. I am acting on inspiration and insights and I trust my inner guidance.
29. I don't play small, I refuse to.
30. I open myself to receiving abundance of the Universe.
31. I have the Midas touch, everything I touch turns to gold.
32. I work where I want, when I want and with people I want to work with.
33. I attract people into my life that help me do big things
34. I set big goals and make a plan for how I am going to accomplish them.
35. When my "why" is strong and clear enough, my "how" appears easily and instantly
36. I always radiate thoughts about my dreams and that helps me attract people and events necessary to achieve them.
37. I celebrate life

38. I have the traits, qualities and mindset to achieve great things in this life.
39. The universe is conspiring on how to bring massive wealth and abundance into my life.
40. I have all that I need right now and keep getting more.
41. Today, inspiration flows easily to me
42. I feel abundant in the here and now.
43. There is nothing in this life I cannot have.
44. I am generous. I help those in need
45. I am attracting prosperity now in expected and unexpected ways.
46. I have unlimited potential.
47. The Universe provides me with all that I will ever need.
48. I understand that giving is as important as receiving and I constantly strive to contribute as much as I can.
49. I am abundant in my finances, in happiness, and in love.
50. I believe in myself fully
51. I find myself in situations and with people who are going to add more to my net worth.
52. My body will feel strong, capable and competent all day.
53. I will set new and inspiring goals today.
54. I am richly blessed.
55. I will find laughter and humor today.
56. I will accept every single person and situation today as is.
57. I surround myself with positive and genuine people who help me and encourage me to reach my goals.
58. I enjoy absolute freedom
59. My confidence is growing more and more each day.
60. The universe has my back
61. I trust the Universe. It gives me exactly what I need at exactly the right time.
62. I am creating a life of passion and purpose.
63. I am love.
64. My attitude will be positive and empowering all day.

65. I have the power to choose my emotional state and I choose a beautiful, happy and successful state ...always
66. Every day I am moving towards my best life.
67. I will attract success and love wherever I go today.
68. I inhale trust and exhale fear
69. My business gets better and better every day.
70. I welcome this day with open arms and thankfulness.
71. I follow bliss. I experience bliss. I am bliss.
72. What I desire and what I ask for is fueled by an unlimited and unwavering belief in myself
73. I step out of my comfort zone to achieve my goals. I find comfort in change and new
74. I will see old relationships get strengthened today and new relationships come into existence today.
75. Everyday I am moving toward my best life
76. New and deeper love will come into my life today.
77. I am One with Spirit
78. My body and mind will overflow with positive energy all day today.
79. I do not believe in rejections, only divine redirections
80. I love myself. I support myself. I believe in myself.
81. Each of my body is awake and charged for a great day.
82. I love myself. I support myself. I believe in myself.
83. I know exactly what I want and constantly remind myself about my goals.
84. My spirit dances in step with joy in my heart.
85. I am divinely guided in all that I do.
86. My intentions are clear, powerful and in complete alignment with my life purpose
87. I use the power of visualization to manifest the life I want
88. I am receiving infinite, inexhaustible and immediate abundance.
89. What I seek is seeking me

90. I think power thoughts! I take power action! I achieve power results
91. I am smart, creative, and motivated. I only take yes for an answer.
92. I have share in the vision of my community and I serve the community with love
93. I am willing to believe that by focusing on feeling good, I make better choices that lead to desired results.
94. I am whole and in perfect health
95. Everything feels so right, and I trust I am on the right path
96. I am wealthy and prosperous in every aspect of my life.
97. I experience the world in all its glory.
98. I am willing to believe that by raising my vibration, I will attract more of what I desire.
99. I constantly think about the thing that I want to attract and this constant thinking attracts the desired thing into my life.
100. I am receiving abundance now in expected and unexpected ways.
101. I am giving and receiving all that is good and all that I desire.
102. Every cell in my body vibrates with health and positive energy.
103. I am attracting more and more wealth and success into my life each day.
104. Whatever I can unify in my mind and my heart I can manifest in my world
105. I am confident of my ability to create the life of my desire and am constantly at it.
106. My life unfolds beautifully before me as I navigate my path with grace and ease
107. My teachers and mentors inspire me to live in the now
108. Each one of my pores radiates with abundance.
109. I transform my mind with the power of visualization
110. I see beauty everywhere I go.

111. I am completely worth of all the good things that life has to offer.
112. I attract an abundance of love and happiness in my current and new relationships.
113. Money and success come into my life so easily and naturally.
114. I am constantly striving to raise my vibration through good thoughts, words and actions.
115. My soul is ready to live the life of my dreams.
116. I attract the life of my desires. I take whatever action necessary for the same.
117. I have deep courage to walk my own path and follow my dreams
118. I am completely ready for my life to overflow with abundance.
119. Each and every day provides me with the perfect mix of sun and rain to grow my dreams into realities
120. In my mind's eye, I see a new and vibrant life for me and attract that life for me.
121. Faith in my future lifts me higher than fear
122. All the pieces of my life are falling perfectly into place now
123. I am constantly and unwaveringly thinking about my goals and thereby attracting them.
124. My life has massive meaning and I am working on leaving a huge legacy.
125. Today is a great day it is to be alive
126. Beauty is the breath of my soul.
127. My dreams correspond to my beliefs and my life corresponds to my dreams.
128. I am creating my life according to my dominant beliefs; and I AM improving the quality of those beliefs.
129. My intentions for my life are clear. What I am seeking is seeking me.

130. I am making a meaningful contribution to the world and I AM wonderfully compensated for my contribution.
131. I am financially wealthy
132. I am attracting all the abundance I desire, fulfilling all my wishes
133. I understand that I and only I am responsible for the quality of my life.
134. I am willing to believe that I am the creator of my life's experiences.
135. I am powerful.
136. My constant thoughts and subsequent actions create my life experiences.
137. My positive attitude always attracts success in whatever endeavour I undertake.
138. I will find adventure in the day today.
139. I will make the best choices today
140. I am a magnet to happiness. I only attract cheerful and happy people in my life.
141. Checks arrive in my inbox every single day.
142. I open myself up to all the wealth and happiness life has to offer.
143. My wisdom will grow today.
144. My gut feeling and the inner guidance that I receive help me inch towards my goal.
145. I am grateful for all that is and all that will be.
146. My wealth grows in ever increasing amounts.
147. I am going to get so much done today.
148. My food and physical activity is such that I attract the best of health.
149. I will manage my time perfectly today.
150. I have developed the habit of feeling good under any circumstances as this helps me in seeing life in a different perspective.
151. I love my blessings

152. I am grateful for_____
153. I greet today with gratitude.
154. I am limitless in my ability to have the things I want in this life.
155. I deserve success, prosperity and happiness and I attract them all.
156. I greet today with excitement and confidence.
157. I attract love everywhere
158. My dreams are much bigger and greater than my fears.
159. I weigh _____ pounds/kgs. And I am happy with it
160. I am always climbing higher and higher in every area of my life.
161. I feel healthy and strong.
162. My life is one big adventure
163. I am surrounded by people who want the best for me and are going to push me to reach my goals and dreams.
164. I am the creator of my own existence and today I choose to create miracles in my life.
165. My mind is completely clear of self doubt, I have unshakable belief in myself.
166. My soul is ready to manifest and live the life of my dreams
167. I am at peace with the world and the world is at peace with me.
168. I will find success and meaning today.
169. My relationships are harmonious
170. I attract positive circumstances and positive people into my life.
171. I trust my journey.
172. My business is a resounding success
173. I am the greatest.
174. I work as and when I want to, anywhere I want to
175. My dreams are coming alive today
176. I am a skilled communicator and I convey my ideas easily. That helps me attract the desired people in my life.

177. My life plays put the way I have envisioned it
178. Today will be a peaceful day.
179. I am exceptionally good at pursuing my dreams
180. I choose to dwell in the realm of possibilities
181. My life is rich and colorful
182. My dreams are manifesting in many ways
183. My success is known in many lands
184. I have witnessed so many personal miracles and I am in a constant state of awe
185. I am doing more than thriving
186. Today, I step into a protective bubble of positivity
187. My life is good
188. I have a wealth of fond memories
189. I can. I will. End of story.
190. My prayers are always answered, in support of my dreams
191. I have the visual insight to see the future that I desire

CHAPTER EIGHTEEN

POSITIVE AFFIRMATIONS FOR MEDITATIONS

1. My mind is clear and focused
2. I can let go of my thoughts at will
3. I value the art of listening.
4. In silent meditation, I can hear the voice of the divine, the beauty of nature, and my own subconscious.
5. A quiet mind brings me peace and happiness.
6. Meditation helps me to see my world and my choices more realistically.
7. My mind is calm even in chaotic times.
8. I monitor my self talk.
9. Kind and loving thoughts guide my speech and actions.
10. Loving others reduces stress in my life
11. I am free from stress and worry
12. If I become tense or irritated, I use my breath to restore my loving thoughts.
13. I look at the world around me and can't help but smile and feel joy.
14. I cherish myself as I breathe in. I cherish others as I breathe out.
15. I admire the good qualities of others.
16. I see that the happiness of others is just as important as my own.
17. By allowing myself to be happy, I inspire others to be happy as well.
18. I refuse to listen to the inner voice that tells me to be afraid.
19. I have the power to stop fear before it takes over.

20. I can tap into a wellspring of inner happiness anytime I wish.
21. My body is relaxed and calm
22. I have a peaceful mind
23. By listening carefully, I learn about myself and the world around me.
24. I feel joy and contentment at this moment right now.
25. I recognize how much I have in common with others.
26. I am happy to accommodate others.
27. Fear is an illusion in the mind, and I know I can overcome it.
28. I listen more than I talk.
29. Loving others strengthens my relationships.
30. I put together a list of all of my fears so I can be on the lookout for them and stop them in their tracks.
31. I am at peace within myself
32. My mind is naturally calm and tranquil
33. Through meditation, I gain insights into my thoughts and behavior.
34. I feel at peace even if things turn out differently than I had planned.
35. If people are discussing something sensitive and I am there, I choose a quiet place and time.
36. I can let go of my fears.
37. I am grateful for my education and health care.
38. My mind is strong and able to see beyond a moment of fear.
39. I may disagree with some of what I hear, but I know that someone may need a chance to express themselves without being judged.
40. If I am unclear about a message, I paraphrase the words of others and ask clarifying questions.
41. I am detached from everything
42. I can detach from all concerns and worries
43. Listening is one way of expressing my concern and respect for others.
44. I appreciate people in the service industry

45. I appreciate the workers who build roads and supply electricity.
46. I clear my mind with meditation and prayer.
47. I recognize my talents and pursue my dreams regardless of any fears that may arise.
48. To generate loving thoughts, I focus on my family and friends.
49. Today, I am free. Free to go after my dreams.
50. Today, I gather information to make sounder decisions.
51. I am committed to my meditation practice
52. My meditation practice is an important part of my life
53. Regardless of my expertise on any topic, I can give someone my attention.
54. My mind is open to the truth about self-imposed limits.
55. I accept that I may sometimes feel uneasy or irritable, but I choose constructive actions that enable me to regain my composure quickly.
56. I avoid creating boundaries for my spirit.
57. Instead of allowing my fears to be in charge, I control my body and mind.
58. I have fun with all of my endeavors, even the most mundane.
59. Fear is an illusion.
60. I leave fears behind and let my creativity blossom.
61. I meditate deeply
62. Meditation comes naturally to me
63. Lending my ear helps me to connect with friends, family, and coworkers on a deeper level.
64. I choose to reduce stress
65. I can avoid panic because I know I am strong and powerful.
66. My mind is a unique vessel that functions without fear.
67. Fear is one of these limits, but I am stronger than the illusion.
68. I am thankful for the kindness of people
69. I am free from the illusion that tries to make me afraid.

70. During difficult times, I listen to my intuition and follow its advice.
71. My mind is at ease
72. Releasing mental tension feels nice
73. I use my ears more than my mouth.
74. I discover more opportunities for building relationships.
75. Remaining calm builds up my strength and confidence.
76. I have the freedom to create the life I desire.
77. I reveal my vulnerabilities.
78. Loving thoughts fill my mind.
79. My intuition guides me to the answers to my issues.
80. I view others with compassion and affection.
81. My thoughts are quiet
82. Meditation improves my health and well-being
83. My ability to listen attentively grows stronger with practice
84. To still my mind, I slow down.
85. My faith in my abilities stabilizes me.
86. Meditation provides calm and clear instructions for action.
87. I stay calm.
88. I choose words that are encouraging and cheerful.
89. I manage my emotions.
90. I find joy and pleasure in the most simple things in life.
91. I am focused on the present moment
92. Mental serenity is mine
93. I hear others out instead of rehearsing what I want to say next.
94. Meditation is a powerful assistant on my journey to happiness.
95. Daily meditations enhances my physical and mental health.
96. I accept feedback graciously.
97. I have a relaxing routine. I take a long walk or a warm bath. I turn off my phone and savor the silence.
98. I remember the good things that people contribute to my life.
99. Downtime makes me more effective.

100. I know the difference between my intuition's voice and my mind's general voice.
101. I will let go of all worries
102. I am naturally gifted at meditation
103. I note two sides of an issue and meditate it over before making decisions
104. I focus on my intuition for guidance.
105. I teach myself to be brave by proving that I can cope with whatever comes my way.
106. I take a step back from the daily rush and collect my thoughts.
107. I step away briefly from a difficult situation to evaluate it.
108. I am able to hear my intuition speak during difficult times.
109. Today, I rejoice in feeling at peace.
110. During meditation, my intuition is given the chance to find answers.
111. My mind is becoming quiet and relaxed
112. During conversations, I avoid interrupting.
113. I reconnect with nature and my friends to help me examine tough situations.
114. I pay attention to my gut feelings and listen to my intuition talk.
115. I face challenges head on and seek solutions calmly
116. Today, I intend to focus on the power of my intuition in a challenging situation.
117. My victories and setbacks become more meaningful because I go through them with family and friends.
118. I am sensitive to the needs of others.
119. I avoid allowing fear to paralyze my intuition or be in charge because I maintain control of challenging situations.
120. I acknowledge all of my feelings, and then focus on the wise whisperings of my inner guide.
121. I am releasing the tension from my body
122. Today, I listen deeply and effectively.

123. My intuition provides valuable lessons about the past, present, and future.
124. Today, I offer my good wishes and practical assistance to those around me.
125. I know the steps I need to take to find success and happiness.
126. My intuition supports me on this journey.
127. If my performance is criticized, I use their feedback to excel the next time.
128. I notice the needs of others and empathize with them in their struggles.
129. I make people feel comfortable as they share their challenges.
130. I surround myself with positive energy.
131. I will focus my mind on the present moment
132. I show my respect and appreciation for others, and gain greater knowledge and wisdom for myself.
133. I love when the energy around me is positive.
134. Meditation makes me feel able to accomplish all I set out to do.
135. I am an observant listener. I pay attention to the tone and voice of the participants during the conversation.
136. Discussions with my friends cover thoughts and plans for a fulfilling future.
137. I make it a point to understand the needs of my family, coworkers, friends, and strangers.
138. I focus on my breath and allow deep breathing to soothe me.
139. I expand my own support group as I support others.
140. Today, I focus on the needs of others. In return, they do the same for me.
141. My meditation practice is improving
142. Today, I also work at listening even when I am alone.

143. I listen to my friends' stories and communicate my concern.
144. Joyfully, my network of friends becomes a circle of love.
145. I help people. I lend a listening ear, offer a shoulder to cry on, and do whatever I can to uplift them.
146. I relax my body and tune out distractions.
147. I notice the minor details while friends talk. This helps me provide wise advice for their situations.
148. I am generous. I share my time and resources freely when they need help.
149. I treat people with kindness and help them work on solutions for a brighter future.
150. I go in search of people, things, and places that exude that positivity and encouragement.
151. I will meditate every day
152. My loved ones know that they can always count on me.
153. Today, I pledge to play my part in bringing positive energy to all situations.
154. I am sensitive to my loved ones' emotional states.
155. When I focus on others, I feel at peace.
156. I understand how to comfort and support people.
157. Positive energy motivates me to achieve important personal objectives.
158. I am full of love and compassion, so my friends know they can turn to me.
159. My commitment to bright and cheery living comes across in all my interactions. I am a positive being.
160. Meditation builds my confidence and willingness to embrace other people's viewpoint.
161. My mind is becoming highly focused and perfectly calm
162. I know I am unable to completely eliminate negativity, but I avoid encouraging it.
163. Whenever I am able to pacify a situation, I take action to calm things down.

164. At times my workplace can be contentious. I remind myself to stay away from conflict.
165. My friendships are based on healthy and supportive communication.
166. It is much easier to focus on my responsibilities when I avoid negative energy.
167. I refrain from judging or criticizing and listen to people with an open heart.
168. The bond I share with my friends helps me to think optimistically.
169. I know that team work produces better results when everyone is on the same page so I encourage it.
170. The positive influence of people sparks ideas.
171. I am finding it easier to detach from my thoughts
172. Meditation helps me to make the most of my opportunities
173. I open my heart before I open my mouth.
174. My sincerity shines in my words
175. I express my true feelings.
176. Today, I practice sincerity. I speak my mind with love
177. I recognize the positive actions and personality traits of others
178. I follow through on what I promise.
179. My words and actions show my friends and family that I am there for them. I listen patiently and validate their experiences
180. I balance criticism with compliments and ask coworkers for their suggestions.
181. I will release all stress and tension when I meditate
182. I live up to my commitments.
183. I earn the trust of others.
184. I provide comfort.
185. I create a calm environment before I deliver criticism that could be difficult to hear.
186. I share constructive feedback.

187. I let my family and friends know how much they mean to me.
188. I focus on collaboration and helping others to enhance their performance.
189. I awaken in the morning feeling happy and enthusiastic about life.
190. I align my mind and thoughts with the intentions of my deepest being
191. Meditation is becoming easier every time I practice

CHAPTER NINETEEN

POSITIVE AFFIRMATIONS FOR BIRTHDAYS

1. Today is the first day of the rest of my life
2. Today, I am worthy and deserving of good things
3. Love is everywhere, and I am loving and lovable.
4. I am a radiant being of love.
5. Today and every day, I do at least one thing that stretches me
6. Struggle is my boot camp preparing for bigger and better things
7. Today I am attracting the people, places, and things that are perfect for my growth
8. Each and every day I reach deeper levels of self-realization.
9. Today what serves me stays and what fails me goes
10. I now see that roadblocks are simply shortcuts to something better than I had planned
11. I am joyous and happy and free.
12. Today I live with a purpose and my purpose lights my path
13. I enter into this new life with ease
14. I trust the process of life to bring me my highest good
15. The obstacles on my path are there to build my strength and understanding.
16. I am a work in progress, but what a work I am!
17. I refuse settle for where I am, when I know I have better within me
18. Today I am taking one step beyond where I have gone before! In no time at all, I'll be far down the road
19. My purpose is to learn to love unconditionally.
20. Today, I love and accept myself exactly as I am.

21. Today, what matters is who I am not who I've been
22. My way forward is paved with the strength of an open heart and the power of an open mind.
23. I experience love wherever I go in this new year
24. Today I am the acorn courageously engaged in the process of becoming the oak
25. I am stronger, wiser and more confident with each new day.
26. I am the captain of my ship. I choose how my days and life unfold.
27. I am now very well organized.
28. I bring my best game to all I do.
29. I now create a wonderful new life
30. I allow myself to receive.
31. My limits yesterday are my starting point today
32. I believe in my talents and skills to make things better wherever I go.
33. Today old paradigms are falling as I find new and better ways to live
34. I am filled with love and affection.
35. My consciousness always expands to embrace the opportunities and challenges in my life
36. Every challenge has called on me to be a better, stronger person and today I am
37. Today I release older lesser versions of myself and grow into my greatness
38. I am in the process of positive changes.
39. I am the best I have ever been
40. I give myself completely to my purpose and my purpose gives me completely to success and happiness.
41. Today I am building bridges from the world that is to the world I choose
42. . I face this challenge with strength and know that I will get through this.
43. In this new life, I flow with life easily and effortlessly.

44. I am following my bliss to inspire others.
45. This season, I pursue my goals with diligence and determination.
46. I have decided that I will enjoy every moment of my life.
47. I intend to live this day to the fullest and practice gratitude.
48. I have a wonderful new relationship with myself
49. I thrive on every opportunity to become more than I have ever been before
50. I now begin a project that will change my life forever – I am unstoppable
51. I pursue peace in all of my relationships.
52. I now move to a better place.
53. I am looking forward to the bright future God has planned for me.
54. I am totally healthy and I am grateful
55. I have the perfect living space.
56. Today I am aware of my desires and intend to pursue them.
57. I declare that I am courageous and brave.
58. Today I exchange my need to always be right for my need to always be growing.
59. I am in a joyous relationship with a partner who deeply loves me.
60. Playing it safe keeps me safe from every dream I have. Today I take risks for my reward
61. I am at peace with others and myself.
62. I go to God first and He directs my steps.
63. I release myself of anger, hate and bitterness – I am free
64. I appreciate all that I do.
65. I have a happy body that pleases me.
66. I choose peace in this situation – I am responsible for my emotions.
67. I embrace fear and self-doubt, not letting anything stop me from what I want.

68. Today I am planting the seeds of growth in my life. I am absolutely committed to watering them every day.
69. Today, I pay attention to my inner longings and act on them.
70. My life is filled with one positive experience after another. I make use of every experience in my growth.
71. I forgive myself from past errors
72. With each breath I take, I feel deeply at peace.
73. Bring the rain. I'm eager to grow! Bring the sunshine. I'm ready to bloom
74. I am co-creating my destiny with my inner wisdom and the universe.
75. Even as I stretch and strive to be who I can be, I am happy with who I am now!
76. I am in love with myself. I love my hair/ nose/ body.
77. This change comes right on time and is exactly what I needed.
78. I use my talents and skills to fulfill my purpose in life.
79. Each and ever day I learn new lessons, expand my awareness, and develop my abilities.
80. I love and accept myself.
81. Today, my thanksgiving extends far beyond my thoughts; I bring a grateful spirit to each step and action I take.
82. I trust myself to be better
83. I may not live forever, but today I strive for better
84. I am eternally young. In mind and body
85. I am grateful now, and that is keeping the door open for more blessings.
86. The universe supports my success
87. Wealth is now my portion. I am prosperous.
88. Today I am the person I came to the planet to be
89. I am on the path to achieving my goals.
90. There is the life that I live and the life that I want. Today I am taking action to bring them into alignment
91. I radiate acceptance.
92. I stand up for myself by saying how I truly feel with kindness.

93. I am my own person.
94. The summit of every success is the foot stool for my next success
95. I thrive on every opportunity to become more than I have ever been before
96. My body is beautiful
97. I now step out of my comfort zone to become the person I believe I can be.
98. Today I'm strong and I understand
99. I feel secure in myself. I am safe.
100. Today I make the most of who I am and what I have to become who I can be
101. Today I am working consciously toward a greater opening of my heart and my mind.
102. Today I am entering new and exciting realms in my life
103. I am strong, courageous and worthy of all good things.
104. I am grateful for my life, the people in it and all that is possible for me.
105. I am full of peace, love and happiness.
106. Every weakness I think I have is an angel whispering, "grow, grow.
107. Everything that happens in my life perfectly prepares me to fulfill my purpose
108. I am ready to make positive change.
109. Today I open my heart to others by seeing the good in them.
110. This week I am breaking new ground in my life and it feels great
111. The past is a blessing because it is my teacher. The future is a blessing because it is my opportunity.
112. I take daily action on things that matter to me.
113. Day by day and thought by thought, I am creating my ideal life
114. Today, I am overflowing with joy, love and gratitude.

115. I celebrate all that is right in the world
116. Today I am liberating myself from the shadows of my past. A bright new day dawns for me
117. New and exciting opportunities are ahead of me – I am creating my destiny.
118. I breathe good thoughts in and breathe bad thoughts out.
119. I release old habits that are limiting my potential.
120. I am grateful for all the good that surrounds me – I attract goodness
121. I am letting go of what I cannot change.
122. Today, I am thankful.
123. I am grateful for the helpful guides that sometimes appear in disguise to usher me back to love.
124. I let go of fear of the past and embrace love and joy the present
125. I forgive myself and release my past.
126. Today I release old habits and blaze new trails
127. In my life, I'm willing to see beauty where others see nothing; I can look beyond a rock and uncover the diamond.
128. I am ready for a healthy, loving and lasting relationship.
129. Today I am aligned with energies that heal my past and grow my future.
130. I am starting fresh by forgiving this person.
131. I deserve love, trust and peace in my life.
132. I forgive for a better life.
133. I struggle, but I grow. I fall, but I get up. Even amid adversity, I succeed and I prosper
134. I give and receive love openly and freely.
135. I welcome all of the ways the universe wants to bless me.
136. On this day, I shine the light of appreciation on an otherwise dark situation; there is no darkness that can escape that light for long.
137. I am brave enough to ask the universe for the life I desire
138. I radiate confidence in all I do

139. Henceforth, I choose to be kind to everyone I encounter – I am kind.
140. I am creating the best possible life for myself and those I love.
141. Today, I can be anything I wish to be.
142. I inspire people with my kind words and actions.
143. I am the master of my destiny
144. I exude kindness and love in my heart.
145. By releasing what is, I open the door for something better
146. Today and every day, I am on a heroic journey from where I am to where I am destined to be
147. I create my own life everyday and I work hard to create a life full of growth and expansion.
148. Abundance comes to me because I am grateful.
149. Today is a new chapter and a fresh start.
150. Each day is a new opportunity to be amazing.
151. I am a magnet for good and for that good… I am grateful.
152. I will create the life that I desire.
153. I am eternally grateful for the love I am capable of giving, and for the love I have yet to receive.
154. I choose to be thankful for the light of this new morning, and for renewed energy and strength to be who I know I can be.
155. This new year, I accept my burdens an I accept my blessings, and so I transform my burdens into my blessings.
156. I partner with peace today, and I do this through the power of keeping a grateful heart.
157. I am willing to trust that my life is exactly as it's meant to be.
158. I choose to see this season of my life, then, through the eyes of appreciation, as best as I can.
159. Whatever has happened, and whatever does happen, I'm certain that I can be grateful again.

160. This year, my thanksgiving is going to be perpetual; it survives every obstacle because I am willing to keep it alive.
161. I am learning to be grateful for what I have while being excited for what has yet to come.
162. I let go of negative confrontations. I choose to see peace instead.
163. I feel profound gratitude for all I am and all I have.
164. Today, my gratitude is an absolute magnet for the manifestation of all that I want
165. I am willing to trust that my life is exactly as it's meant to be.
166. Regardless of whatever I see, I trust that the universe is supporting my highest good.
167. I know gratitude is a daily choice and today, I choose to be grateful.
168. I can relax a little and be thankful for what I have now.
169. Gratitude opens the door for my essence to flow through my life, and spirit blessings to
170. Today marks the beginning of a new dispensation in my life
171. I fully accept the joy that wants to surface in my life, and I accept it now in gratitude.
172. I just feel grateful this morning.
173. I am attracting good into my life.
174. I am grateful and thankful for all goodness God has given me.
175. Starting today, my daily attitude is one of gratitude.
176. I give thanks daily for blessings that flow into my life.
177. For the rocks and the diamonds, I am thankful, because life is a rich experience that includes everything.
178. I am grateful for my life and growing consciousness within it
179. I realize that I am blessed in so many ways and am deeply grateful

180. I am feeling that I have a grateful heart.
181. The feeling of gratefulness expands my perspective and opens me up to new ways of living happily in this world; it's as if the whole universe is in my heart.
182. I am grateful.
183. The more grateful I am, the more blessed I am.
184. My soul continuously rejoices and unites with my experience as I engage in gratitude.
pour into all that I choose to create.
185. I see abundance all around me. I am grateful.
186. I see the benefits of gratitude. I now immerse in gratitude and cultivate it as a habit.
187. I am grateful for my health.
188. I am shining brighter and brighter unto perfection
189. This year, I am doing great exploits
190. I rise triumphantly with grace
191. By my gratitude, I am close to the source of abundance.

CHAPTER TWENTY

POSITIVE AFFIRMATIONS FOR THE TRAVELLER

1. I enjoy peace and tranquility on my dream holiday.
2. I am taking a trip to the most amazing holiday destination in the world.
3. I am constantly marveling at the worlds many wonders.
4. Incredible things are headed my way.
5. I deserve the happiness that this new start offers to me.
6. I am grateful for the opportunity to travel the world.
7. I will create sunshine for the joy of others.
8. I always spread joy and love wherever I go.
9. I am lucky for the opportunity of a fresh start, full of love and laughter.
10. The best is yet to come.
11. I attract the vacation of my dreams.
12. There is no limit to what I can do or to the love I can receive.
13. My bags are packed and I am ready to go.
14. I live and breathe excitement and seek out new experiences.
15. I release harmful thoughts of my past and look to the future with excitement.
16. I am in charge of the trajectory of my adventurous spirit.
17. I visit lands far and wide while discovering the world.
18. Through travel, I learn to embrace happiness in the largest and smallest of places.
19. I am happy with the me I am right now in this moment.
20. I face the challenges of today with a positive and cheerful spirit.
21. The perfect trip away is within my grasp.

22. Money for travel flows into my life effortlessly.
23. I walk into this situation expecting love and openness.
24. I am the happiest I have ever been.
25. I am open to receiving an abundance of love and wild adventure.
26. Taking time out for rest and relaxation at a beautiful resort is where I am meant to be.
27. The more love I give to my endeavors, the more I receive.
28. I sail the deepest oceans and fly over the highest mountains to reach my dream destination.
29. I am so grateful for the opportunity of knowing a new home.
30. I invite new opportunities into my life.
31. I visualize my dream holiday every day.
32. I am prepared to prosper beyond my wildest dreams.
33. I enjoy the company of my loved ones while enjoying my dream vacation.
34. I appreciate my abundant life.
35. I am a magnet for new journeys and adventures.
36. My desire for new experiences inspires others to break free.
37. My getaway is calling me closer each and every day.
38. I am open and willing for new adventures.
39. I give back to the world as love flows into me.
40. Every day holds new opportunities for great things to happen.
41. A fabulous vacation is being drawn toward me.
42. I feel grateful to be able to manifest my dream vacation.
43. Travel teaches me to look on the bright side.
44. Today, I am grateful for all the good things in my life and for those yet to come.
45. Travel makes everything seem
46. Today I choose to let go of all past negative influences.
47. I have unlimited choices.
48. I am the energy that I wish to attract.
49. Travel fills my days with laughter.
50. I find pleasure in the hidden and most secret of places.

51. My dream vacation is on its way.
52. I am grateful for this journey. I am enough, and I have enough.
53. I wake up in a new place joyful and inspired to make this day great.
54. The universe provides me with unlimited resources to be able to travel where I want and when I want on my dream vacation.
55. I am grateful for every single one of my adventures and opportunities to grow.
56. I am free to design the life of my dreams, and my imagination knows no limits.
57. I live life to the fullest.
58. The past holds no power over me.
59. I welcome adventure into my life.
60. I greet all life with love in my heart.
61. I indulge in luxury relaxation packages while on my dream vacation.
62. Travel cultivates cheer in me every day.
63. I have all that I need and more.
64. I am open to new and exciting adventures.
65. Travel makes me an optimist.
66. I create the life I deserve.
67. I ask, I believe, I receive.
68. I am surrounded by beauty.
69. Every day in every way, travel is making me happier and happier.
70. Travel makes me radiate positive energy.
71. I am waking up to another relaxing day in paradise.
72. I am worthy of everything good that comes my way and I will accept it with gratitude.
73. I am grateful and open to the abundances of the universe.
74. I attract success and wild adventure.

75. My dream holiday destination draws closer to me each and every day.
76. My heart seeks a journey.
77. Travel helps me to inhale with positivity and peace and exhale negative thoughts.
78. The universe will provide me with adventure and love.
79. Others are attracted to my adventurous spirit.
80. My world is brimming over with joy and love.
81. My energetic signature is an exact match with a wonderful holiday.
82. I allow the abundance of the universe to flow through me.
83. I am worthy of adventure and love in all its forms.
84. I visualize unpacking my bags in the most beautiful location in the world.
85. I simply decide to be excited for the day.
86. I celebrate this life
87. I commit myself to take well deserved holidays often.
88. I always have what I need when I need it in my adventurous heart.
89. All of my dreams are coming true.
90. I am expanding on my cultural awareness while discovering the world.
91. I invest in myself wholeheartedly.
92. The stresses of life all melt away when I vacay in paradise.
93. I graciously accept gifts of the universe with gratitude.
94. I am flying to faraway lands full of excitement.
95. My gratitude knows no limit.
96. I was born to fulfill my travel dreams.
97. A well-deserved break leaves me feeling rested and renewed.
98. The universe loves to show me it's beautiful landscape as I travel around the globe.
99. I am allowed to prosper and accept abundance into my world.
100. As I allow more abundance and love into my life, more doors will open for me.

101. I am jet-setting around the globe.
102. Wealth of the world flows freely into my life.
103. I am creating a life of adventure and happiness.
104. I will not be limited.
105. My happiness grounds me and I allow my fears to drift away.
106. Something incredible is going to happen to me on this trip
107. I visualize eating at the finest restaurants while on my dream holiday.
108. I attract positive events and opportunity into my life.
109. I am carving out the wild and true lifestyle I desire.
110. A river of perfect wealth always runs toward me, washing over me.
111. I am grateful for this journey and the exquisite beauty it brings to my life.
112. I know everything will work out how it should.
113. The downtime I deserve is granted to me in the form of a beautiful getaway
114. Adventure makes me strong and peaceful.
115. I am the architect of my travel fortune.
116. Travel teaches me courage and to embrace my vulnerability.
117. I enjoy sightseeing while taking amazing trips to exotic land.
118. My journeys are always safe, relaxing and enjoyable experiences.
119. I am so very full of peace and gratitude for this journey.
120. I am an adventurous spirit who experiences the Earth's wonders daily.
121. I enjoy plenty of spending money while on holiday in my dream destination.
122. I am so very full of peace and gratitude for this journey.
123. I feel fulfilled for I am certain that all my travel desires are being met.

124. I am deeply fortunate to be in the position to travel.
125. I deserve a long break away from work.
126. I am a traveler.
127. My spirit is pure adventure.
128. The path that I take today leads me to a place of fulfillment and greatness

CHAPTER TWENTY-ONE

POSITIVE AFFIRMATIONS ABOUT EMOTIONS

1. Today, I dig deep into my soul to discover the source of any resentment that accumulates in my heart.
2. I am able to block resentment from feeding on my thoughts and feelings. I release it back into the universe and replace it with positive thoughts.
3. I understand how to discuss my feelings.
4. I can express my emotions with confidence.
5. Meditation shows me how to be content and relaxed.
6. I tune out emotional distractions and focus on creating balance.
7. My concentration on my real feelings grow stronger. I pay attention to how my mind works. I listen to my inner voice.
8. I choose to be in control of my actions instead of operating emotionally on autopilot.
9. I remember that I am in control and I have a choice.
10. I focus on my core values and spiritual purpose to keep me grounded
11. I connect with my true emotions.
12. I put aside any form of judgments and regard myself with compassion.
13. Every single day, I make the decision to love and accept myself just the way I am.
14. I recognize the power I have over my life and I decide how to respond to whatever circumstances come my way.
15. I devote my time and emotions to activities that are meaningful to me.

16. I am fully aware of myself and my worth. I know that I am worthy of love and success.
17. I realize that observing my thoughts and feelings about certain things, prepares me to live the life I really want.
18. I cultivate a sense of inner calm and serenity that I can carry with me through traffic jams or tense business meetings without breaking down emotionally
19. I give myself the gift of freedom from resentment. I let go of anger, forgive others, and make room for love.
20. I embrace my feelings and begin the process of healing.
21. I live my life mindfully and deliberately.
22. I define myself in a way that goes beyond my age, gender, profession or even past experiences
23. When things start to get frantic, I slow down and breathe deeply.
24. I am ready to put in the work to overcome obstacles.
25. I understand the power of resentment and its ability to harm my mind and body. Therefore, I work actively on letting go
26. I set aside time for meditation and prayer to nourish me emotionally
27. Today, I tackle challenges without overwhelming myself with too many responsibilities.
28. I take a walk outdoors to enjoy nature to relax myself and connect with my center.
29. My relationships remain secure while I express my thoughts and feelings
30. My center is a source of strength that gives me the determination to persevere.
31. To let go of past hurt, I focus my awareness on the present moment.
32. In chaos, I reach for my center. To connect with my center, I still my mind.
33. I find the source of my resentment so I can let it go.
34. By staying centered, I can accept the natural changes in life.

35. I am living in the present
36. My center is strong and this is the place where I feel in balance emotionally.
37. I attract calming situations and people into my life
38. I am confident when I'm around others
39. I clarify my thoughts as I sieve through my emotions. My mind slows down.
40. I trust in my inner wisdom
41. I control my emotional outbursts and at the same time, I experience the stability that comes with being in touch with my authentic self.
42. I release anxiety because I know it is just passing through
43. Today, I gladly let go of any resentment in my heart and move forward toward a happy life without this negative emotion.
44. I replace feelings of worry with hope
45. I identify with my feelings of anxiety as much as I do peace
46. I look deeper than the surface. I see beyond superficial labels and roles.
47. I am capable of adjusting to new situations
48. I am confident in my future
49. My confidence, inner wisdom and self esteem increase daily
50. I refuse to allow the pain of resentment to fester inside me.
51. I am more than my genetics
52. I react to my anxiety calmly and effectively
53. I inhale confidence and exhale self doubt
54. I learn from my anxiety
55. I learn strategies that I can use to release negative emotions in a healthy way and I practice them daily.
56. I know my intuition is my best guide
57. I know that being direct is the most effective approach so, imbibe it.
58. I vibrate at a higher emotion than anxiety
59. I interpret my emotions and have the final say in how I react

60. I release habits of worry
61. I reduce the risk of misunderstandings and delays by keeping communication clear
62. I embrace stress, it steers me away from what drains me
63. My beliefs and values create a strong foundation for my life. I am centered and grounded.
64. I am courageous and confront my fears
65. To maintain balanced communications, I ask myself what would serve the common good rather than just my own interests.
66. I ask for what I want.
67. I face difficult situations with courage
68. I am more than my family history of mental illness
69. I am proactive. To help me let go of resentment, I study positive communication methods.
70. Meditation gives me an opportunity to discover my true self.
71. To put myself in a sincere frame of mind, I examine my motives.
72. I allow myself to be vulnerable and this deepens my relationships.
73. I check that my thoughts are free from resentments and anxiety.
74. Meditation helps me to unleash my true emotions as well as my true potential.
75. My toxic self-doubts fad away.
76. I have the ability to create change in my life.
77. I let go of the past for it no longer serves me.
78. Where I am mentally and emotionally is OKAY
79. As I release stress and anxiety, my mind grows still and peaceful.
80. I speak only positive things.
81. I choose to respond to emotions that build me.
82. I stop comparing myself to others, and work on leveraging my own unique strengths.

83. I do not indulge in self pity.
84. I can also let go of bitterness because I understand that my past can only affect my present or future if I let it.
85. I enjoy the emotional journey I am on. I love who I am becoming.
86. I approve of myself.
87. I am my own rock emotionally
88. I am a warrior and a soldier when it comes to protecting my mental health
89. I have no fear of my future.
90. I am in love with this life so much
91. I am completely fearless as I discover the real me
92. I am a gift to the world.
93. Today, I cultivate a strong center that guides my decisions, my actions and my reactions.
94. I am not oppressed. There is no mountain I can't climb.
95. I like how far I have come emotionally. I am an inspiration to others.
96. I make the choice is to learn what I can from unfortunate situations, leave them in the past, and move forward without them.
97. I love myself fully and completely.
98. I love and approve of myself.
99. I am brave and grateful to have learned it.
100. I surround myself with positive vibes and allow travel to lift my spirits.
101. I choose to be relaxed and happy.
102. Today, I sit down to meditate. I explore my feelings and learn to appreciate myself.
103. I will not stress over things I can't control.
104. I pause and reflect before reacting.
105. I am superior to negative thoughts.
106. I let go of all the worries that drain my energy and feel as light as a feather.

107. I accept and embrace all experiences.
108. I am becoming more calm, positive and loving everyday
109. My happiness is contagious.
110. I prove to myself that daily that happiness comes from within rather than depending on material possessions or approval from others.
111. I am centered, peaceful, and grounded.
112. I am surrounded by supportive loved ones always.
113. Today is a good day.
114. I am content and at peace.
115. Negative thoughts are not me.
116. I invite peace into all my interactions with others.
117. I am peacefully allowing this moment to pass.
118. I am happy right here, right now.
119. I am grateful for this moment.
120. I am complete, with nothing to prove.
121. I am not alone.
122. I am gentle with my words and my thoughts.
123. I observe my emotions with calm detachment.
124. I do not judge my own thoughts.
125. I forgive myself for past mistakes.
126. I am alive in this moment.
127. My heart is bursting with joy.
128. My mind is at ease.
129. I choose to be calm.
130. I am here, now.
131. I allow my soul to shine.
132. I discard all expectations.
133. I am peaceful in my place.
134. I find joy in stillness.
135. I am calm and content.
136. Today is fresh and new.
137. I am in charge of how I feel.
138. I am in control of my emotions and feelings today

139. I exude warmth and kindness.
140. I am pure sunshine.
141. I focus on what I can control and I let go of what I can't.
142. I love my beautiful mind.
143. I am allowed to have bad days.
144. I am a survivor and that makes me proud of myself.
145. I have a beautiful laugh.
146. I stay calm in frustrating situations
147. I invest in myself through big and small acts of self-care and self-love.
148. I am brave to endure emotional days like today.
149. Life is tough sometimes, but so am I.
150. My smile makes others smile.
151. I am choosing love over other emotions
152. My inner strength knows no bounds
153. I am patient with and kind to myself.
154. I look forward to feeling better about things again.
155. I am proud of the person I am today, and the person I will be tomorrow.
156. I am in control of my emotions
157. I breathe in energy and love, I exhale negativity and doubt.
158. Life is tough sometimes, but so am I.
159. Tomorrow is more than another day; it's another chance to shine.
160. I rock at being me!
161. I am attracting the love my heart desires
162. I look after my mental health because it deserves my love
163. My bad days and unhappy moments will always pass.
164. I am trusting in my ability to set myself free
165. I bring joy to the world.
166. I choose my peace of mind
167. I'm not ashamed or alone in having mental health struggles.

168. I can see the end of this emotional time, and I move towards it with every breath I take.
169. I am attracting kindness from others
170. My hugs are full of love and warmth.
171. When chaos surrounds me, I remain calm
172. My mental health is just as important as my physical health.
173. I take time to know my needs, limits and boundaries better.
174. I am attracting people who treat me well
175. Love is what I believe in most of all.
176. I am manifesting love and happiness from within
177. Good mental health is a journey, not a destination.
178. On hard days like this, I love myself more than ever.
179. I am making responsible decisions
180. I sow seeds of peace wherever I go
181. I inspire others to be happy when I allow myself to be happy
182. I open my heart to healing
183. I breathe in peace and breathe out dysfunction
184. I grow more at peace each day
185. My good days prepare me for my harder days
186. I stay calm in frustrating situations
187. I am processing my hurt and anger in healthy ways
188. I surround myself with people who care about my wellbeing
189. Life is tough sometimes, but I am tougher
190. I am considerate of how my decisions affect others
191. My heart is full of love for who I am.

www.ingramcontent.com/pod-product-compliance
Lightning Source LLC
Chambersburg PA
CBHW031110080526
44587CB00011B/915